# Thinking Things Through

*General Editors*
**Graham Slater and C. S. Rodd**

## 10. Prayer

GW00630907

Thinking Things Through

# Thinking Things Through

## 10. Prayer

Stephen B. Dawes

EPWORTH PRESS

ISBN 0-7162-0555-6


First published 2003
by Epworth Press
4 John Wesley Road,
Peterborough
PE4 6ZP


Printed and bound by
Biddles Ltd
Guildford and King's Lynn

# Contents

# General Introduction

The great Swiss theologian, Hans Küng, has said that his aim in all his writings is to enable his readers to hold their faith with confidence and not with a bad conscience. This new series, prompted by the conviction that Christians need to think through their faith but often lack appropriate help in so doing, has a similar aim. Moreover, the assistance that it seeks to offer is related to another conviction: that many church members need persuading that theologians are concerned in any way with their problems and that theology can be at all relevant to their lives.

In such a situation, it is essential, we are sure, to begin with life and with church life. Only in that way can we be confident that we are dealing with grassroots issues. Plainly, however, it is not enough to identify the questions where they arise; we must also indicate the sources of help – if not of all the answers – in as non-technical a way as possible.

In some volumes, these tasks will be tackled in sequence; in others, they will be interwoven. Whatever the precise format, however, our hope is that, through this interaction, difficulties will be faced, fears dispelled, open discussion promoted, and faith informed and strengthened.

The books can either be read by individuals on their own or used in groups. We hope the questions at the end of each chapter will be useful both as a check that the text has been understood and as a spur to reflection and discussion.

Later volumes will deal with Jesus and the Holy Spirit.

GRAHAM SLATER AND C. S. RODD

# Introduction

The spirituality industry is booming at the moment, as any look at the 'Mind, Body and Spirit' section of an Ottakers or a Waterstones will tell you. Many of the books on these shelves are books about prayer, though they more usually call it meditation, focusing, centring or 'transformation'. In the much smaller 'Religious' section you will also find a mini-book going on in books of prayers, of all types and for all ages, many featuring the current craze-word 'Celtic' in their titles. Both outside and inside organized Christianity, it seems, prayer is alive and well.

At the same time, however, I hear and have heard for most of my thirty years in ministry that 'Prayer is a problem'. Personal prayer is something we know we should do, but don't do as well or as much as we think we should. Prayer in worship can be magnificent, inspiring and enlightening, but usually isn't. In both cases I speak personally as well as on behalf of those many who have shared such feelings with me over the years.

This little book is not a guide to books of prayers, nor a 'how to' kind of book on how to pray better or even how to pray at all. In line with the other books in this series, it looks at the problems faced by real people in 'thinking through' prayer and issues about prayer, not least the intellectual and theological issues which lie behind the problems which many have with prayer. In it we listen in to Sue as she shares her confusion about how prayer 'works', and we see how this generates conversations, sometimes heated ones, in and around the House Group at her church. As the conversations flow and spark it becomes clear that at the heart of many of the questions which grip Sue and her friends is the unavoidable question, what kind of a God is it with whom we try to engage or who is trying to engage with us? Those questions shape the second half of the book.

I am grateful to the Epworth Press for the unexpected invitation to write this particular book, and for the encouragement of Gerald Burt and the Series Editors as it took shape. I am also more indebted than I can say to the folks of the churches and chapels among whom I have ministered and to the students in colleges and on courses whom I have taught, from all of whom I have received so much. If this book helps one or two of them to hold to faith with greater confidence, then that will be an 'answer to prayer', for Vincent if not for Geoff. So please, read on.

STEPHEN B. DAWES

# Part 1

# Conversations

# 1
## A Conversation over Coffee

Trepolpen United Church (Church of England, United Reformed and Methodist) is one of those churches where coffee is served in the revamped foyer after morning service. Some of the congregation sit around with their friends, some move from group to group chatting about this and that, and some get straight off home to make sure Sunday lunch is ready. Today's service is over, nicely within the hour, and Sue is telling her friends Jo and Christine what she heard this morning on Pause for Thought on Radio Ourshire.

She usually listens to this three-minute slot on the local radio station each Sunday morning, and often gets something from it. But today's programme was somehow different, and she wasn't sure what she made of it. The speaker was someone she knew. He had been the visiting preacher at their Harvest Festival a year or two before and he often spoke on the radio. He was someone she enjoyed listening to, someone she trusted. But what he had said this morning had made her think – she knew that that was no bad thing – but it had also made her slightly anxious. And she wasn't quite sure why. So she was telling Jo and Christine about it.

This is what she had heard:

Good morning everyone, this is John Smith, your farming vicar, with today's Pause for Thought, two days before the start of the Royal Ourshire Agricultural Show. I go every year and, as usual, people have been saying to me 'Pray for good weather for the Show, John'.

Sorry folks, can't do that. It's just like praying for a safe journey home from the studio. Can't do that either. The weather for the Show's going to happen like it's going to happen, no matter what you want, I want, or God wants. And whether I get home safely today depends on how I drive and how everybody else on the road drives. What God

3

wants – which is for all of us to be safe on the road – doesn't come into it.

I can, of course, pray for patience and consideration in my driving and for the gumption to watch my speed and drive carefully, but any other sort of prayer is just silly. Life's not like that and neither is religious faith. So if you're coming to the Show – and I hope you are – bring your mac, just in case. Bye for now.

As Sue tells them what she remembers of the broadcast, Christine listens attentively. She enjoys a good discussion about Christianity, about most things really, and can't wait for Sue to finish so that she can chip in. Jo is the opposite. She comes to church, enjoys the worship, gets involved in some of the social events and is always ready to help with the tea, the crèche or the cleaning. Even the Christian Aid house-to-house collection if they're desperate. But she's not at all sure what Sue is getting at and doesn't really want to know. This kind of conversation makes her uncomfortable. She is glancing at the clock, waiting for the moment in which it would be polite to say she has to go now.

The moment has come, and Jo has gone. Christine, a bright thirty-something who has recently qualified as a lay preacher, is making it quite clear to Sue that she thinks the Farming Vicar is spot-on. The idea of praying for good weather went out with the Middle Ages, she insists. And the idea of God arranging the weather according to how many prayers he gets or what kind is nonsense! Besides, doesn't a farmer want rain on one field and sun on the next at the same time? How is God expected to cope with that?

It's easy to laugh, Sue thinks, but doesn't say. She can't put her niggling feelings into words. Something inside her doesn't want to admit that Christine and the Farming Vicar might be right. It makes God sound so – what's the right word? – helpless. Yes, helpless. And if God really can't change things or help with things, then what is faith and worship all about? And why do we pray at all?

Then, coffee cup in hand, Mary arrives. She is the lay preacher who has led the worship that morning. She had seen the little group of young mums in the corner earlier, but had been waylaid by a talkative visitor as she was making her way to join them. Despite that, she has been able to overhear much of their conversation. Christine never was quiet. She also noticed the look of relief on Jo's face as she slipped away. Escaping from the visitor, she decides to take pity on Sue, for she knows Christine's lively mind and strong arguments from discussions in the Preachers' Meeting. Besides, she wants to get involved.

Christine finishes what she was saying to Sue and summarizes it for Mary, who is obviously interested. 'Would that be worth talking about in the House Group?', Mary asks. Yes, it would, thinks Sue, who rarely says anything in the House Group but has got a lot from it in the two years she has been attending, 'Yes, it would', says Christine, always ready to talk about anything, anywhere.

*Questions for discussion*

1. The Farming Vicar's radio talk made Sue feel uneasy. What are your immediate reactions to his talk?

2. The Farming Vicar doesn't believe that prayer makes any difference to the weather. Does prayer or praying, in your experience, make any difference to anything?

3. What are the issues about prayer which you hope this book will help you to think through?

What is it appropriate 5 to prayer for?

Is god limited - 'helpless'?

# 2
## A Stormy House Group

Andrew, Mary's husband, has done his usual thing. Tonight the House Group is holding its monthly meeting in their lounge, so he has prepared the coffee and biscuits, welcomed the dozen or so people who come, put the coats on the spare bed, and withdrawn to the loft to work on his model railway.

Mary, who leads the group most months, has done some homework. She has phoned John Smith, the Farming Vicar, and asked him for a copy of the script of the Radio talk that had made Sue feel uneasy. His response had been even better than she had expected: he had sent her a tape of it.

Mary's House Group, as they all call it, has an open programme. Usually, since it's the sort of group that tries to scratch where people are itching and most of the members are happy to bring issues to be shared, they decide what to do at the beginning of each meeting. This means that, occasionally, they follow up something which has arisen at the previous meeting. This month, though, they have nothing like that planned, and so Mary, after she has welcomed everyone and led them in a short gathering prayer and a longer centring silence, shares her suggestion that they discuss the Farming Vicar's radio talk. No one has any other suggestions.

Having experienced all too many technological disasters in church, Mary has prepared properly. She has checked in advance that the machine is working, that the tape fits, and that the volume is set right. So the group is delivered both from anxiety that the tape-recorder may not work and from embarrassing attempts at repairs when it doesn't. Mary presses the button on the zapper and they hear, 'Good morning everyone, this is . . . '

They listen. The tape stops. Mary invites them to be quiet for a moment or two to reflect on what they have heard.

When discussion begins, Geoff jumps in straightaway. 'That's exactly what's wrong with the church', he says. 'Vicars who don't believe in the power of prayer and then go round telling people they don't. No wonder the churches are empty.' By contrast, he tells them, he himself firmly believes in the power of prayer. And it works. He prays for journeying mercies every time he takes his car out of the garage. And he prays for a parking space every time he comes into town, and God always answers his prayer.

After that outburst, conversation quickly becomes very animated!

Christine jokes that Geoff s kind are those who pester God as if he's got nothing better to do than to look after them and meet their needs, however trivial those needs might be. And as for 'journeying mercies', she can just about remember her granny praying for those and that was centuries ago, but that might have been because of granddad's driving . . .

Geoff comes straight back. He is serious. He believes that God answers prayer, and that God is so interested in every part of our lives that nothing is too small or insignificant to bring to him in prayer. Nor is any part of life too trivial for him to care about.

Christine sees that the time for joking is over. So she asks Geoff what he thinks he has got eyes and hands and a brain for? And, before he can answer, she tells him. They are gifts from God for him to use to find his own parking space when he drives into town. Then she moves on. What is really wrong with Geoff's point of view, she argues, is that it is fundamentally unfair, even unjust. It paints the wrong picture of God and sends out the wrong signals about him. It makes him partial. Praying people are his favourites and he gives them special deals. He might make his sun shine on the good and the bad alike, and his rain fall on the just and the unjust, but when it comes to parking spaces there's one law for those who pray and another for the rest. Is that it? As far as she is concerned, that is 'insurance policy prayer' at its worst. She couldn't believe in God at all, she says, if she thought there was a shred of truth in what Geoff is saying.

7

The rest of the group are a bit stunned. Lively discussions are one thing, but this has almost become a violent argument. Some begin to take sides. Others try to defuse things a bit. Someone asks Geoff if it's really true that he gets a parking space every time. Someone else says that he's just lucky, that it's a happy coincidence that someone is always leaving just as he's arriving. Someone else says that it really is time the Council built a bigger car park anyway. Someone asks Christine about what she thinks it is right to pray for. Someone else says that she must be very brave if she never sends up a little prayer when she's driving round the ring road in the rush hour. Someone else reminds them all that praying for things or for people is after all only one kind of prayer and that there are others.

Sue says nothing all evening. She doesn't pray like Geoff does, and thinks that his way of praying does sound rather, well, childish. But she is also worried by Christine's response. Surely God is interested in each of us? What about that hymn which says he 'delights to meet fresh needs'? And doesn't Jesus say things like 'Ask and you will receive', and 'How much more will your Heavenly Father give good things to those who ask him"? She is more confused than ever. She wishes she'd never listened to the radio that Sunday morning and never said anything about it to Christine and Jo at church.

Geoff goes home muttering about Christine and all the other semi-believers who do so much damage to the church. Christine goes home muttering about Geoff and how much harm he and those who are as naïve as he is do to the church.

Mary has a sleepless night. The evening hadn't gone right at all. She knows that. It hadn't been a discussion. It had been an argument. Nobody had listened to anybody else. Nobody had tried to get behind the words and the feelings. Perhaps they had started at the wrong place? The radio talk had been about what it is right or wrong to pray for. Perhaps that's not the right place to have begun? But that was precisely the question that had been bugging Sue. Someone had said at the end that there is much more to prayer than praying for things. Mary knew that intercession is only one kind of prayer, but she also knew that it is an important one and a difficult one. After all, it was because it bugged her too that she herself had made the suggestion about tonight,

But one thing was clear to Mary. It was that for both Geoff and Christine this issue had touched a nerve. It was not just a question of how to pray or what to pray for. Nor a question of what prayer is and how it works. Was it a deeper question of what God is like and what having faith in him means? It almost looked as if Geoff and Christine believed in two rather different Gods.

She consoled herself with the thought that the evening couldn't have been a total disaster. If it had been, the group members wouldn't have committed themselves to carrying on the conversation next time, would they?

## Questions for discussion

1. The words of Jesus in Matthew 7.7, 'Ask and you will receive, seek and you will find, knock and the door will be opened to you', strongly suggest that prayer will be answered. What are your views on this question which so bitterly divided Mary's House Group?

2. The words of the hymn which Sue is thinking about are from the last line of the fourth verse of 'Come, all who look to Christ today' by Richard G. Jones (*Hymns and Psalms* 765). The whole verse reads:

> Bring your traditions' richest store,
>     Your hymns and rites and cherished creeds;
> Explore our visions, pray for more,
>     Since God delights to meet fresh needs.

9

What is prayer about – things or something else?
What kind of God are we praying to?

What do you think that last line means when you read the rest of the verse, especially the third line?

3. Mary is beginning to think that Geoff and Christine believe in different Gods. Is it starting to look as if how we pray and what we pray for depend on the picture we have of God? What picture of God do you have when you pray?

# 3
## Walking the Dog

You don't have to have a dog to be a member of Mary's House Group – but it helps. Vincent (King Charles Spaniel, full pedigree) and Sarah (terrier plus collie plus several unidentifiable bits – all in the same dog) often walk their dogs together on the Common.

'Vincent.'

'Yes, Sarah?'

'Last night made me a bit uncomfortable . . . '

'Mmm?'

'Well, it's not easy to talk about is it?'

'What isn't?'

'Prayer, of course.'

'Suppose not.'

'How do you pray, then?'

'Two *Hail Marys*, night and morning'

'Pardon?'

'"Holy Mary, Mother of God, pray for us sinners now and at the hour of our death, Amen". Twice. Night and morning. In bed.'

'In bed? Not in a quiet time or anything like that?'

'No. In bed.'

'Do you have a quiet time or anything like that?'

'No.'

'You don't have a time when you sit down and think and pray and read the Bible and things like that?'

'No, Sarah. Why? Do you think I should have?'

'Well, Christians do, don't they? I mean, aren't we all supposed to pray every day and read the Bible every day? That's why they sell the Bible Reading Notes at church, isn't it? And the Prayer Handbook?'

'That's what we were always taught at St Agathas – well, the saying your prayers bit anyway; but I don't know how many folks do or don't. I suppose old Father Alfred wouldn't be amused at my quick *Hail Marys* night and morning.'

'But you say them.'

'Yes, I say them.'

'Oh.'

'Sarah, do you have a problem here? You used the "supposed" word. Are you saying that you think you're supposed to pray every day and read the Bible every day, but you don't?'

'Yes. No. I mean Yes. Yes, I think I'm supposed to; and No, I don't actually do it. Not every day, anyway.'

'And you feel bad about it?'

'Sometimes.'

'Sometimes?'

'Sometimes. Especially when I'm with some of the group, like Mary and Liz, and specially Geoff. I think they'd be horrified if they knew about it. You're not horrified?'

'It takes a lot to horrify this lapsed Catholic.'

'But you pray night and morning?'

'Two *Hail Marys* between putting the light off and going to sleep isn't quite enough to get you canonized, even these days when we get a new saint every other week.'

'Have you never felt bad about it?'

'Yes, I have. Just like I felt bad when I stopped going to Mass every week. But I was a teacher. My job was trying to get young people to think for themselves.'

'Oh, that sort of teacher.'

'Yes, that sort of teacher. Just like you. I was a teacher, Sarah, trying to get youngsters to think, and eventually I realized that I needed some space to think for myself. Still do. But if we're into sharing confession time, I go into St Dominic's Cathedral every time I go into the city, and that's once a week most weeks. And I sit there, in that holy place, just sit. "Sometimes I sits and thinks and sometimes I just sits".'

'Huckleberry Finn.'

'Indeed. Just sit, but it's getting to mean a lot.'

'My just-sitting place is over there. The seat by the fir tree.'

'Ah . . . '

'But often I sit and read. Especially prayers, little books of prayers and meditations. Jim Cotter. Iona. I even hum the odd Taizé chant.'

'Can't stand them. Even though they're in Latin, they're still ditties.'

'Vincent!'

'Sorry.'

'Yes, I sit and read. Sometimes. Not always. I suppose what we're both doing is "centring". Isn't that what the women's magazines call it? Not quite meditating or anything like that, but "Be still and know that I am God". That sort of thing?'

'I suppose it is. What do you do when it rains?'

'Oh, I don't do it every day or anything like that. But yes, if it rains and I need my space – I suppose I am really talking about a sort of quiet time, aren't I? – I call into St Ethelbertha's. It's one of the few churches around these days which are unlocked, and you'd be surprised how often you see somebody else just sitting. Thank you, Vincent.'

'Thank you?'

'Thank you, Vincent, for listening. Thank you for helping me say what I haven't said before, for helping me look at what I do and not feel guilty about what I don't do. Thank you'

'Er . . . No problem. "Pray as you can, not as you can't", somebody or another said once.

Perhaps that's what we both do? Bye then'

'Bye'

*Questions for discussion*

1. There is much guilt around prayer, and it may be difficult, if not impossible, to share in being 'honest about praying' in a group. But Vincent helps Sarah to be honest with herself about it. How honest with yourself are you about your 'prayer life'?

2. Sarah suggests that she and Vincent have been practising 'centring'. Consider ways in which you might practise it.

3. Do you have a 'sitting place'? If you have, talk about it to the rest of the group.

The practice of prayer
Guilt about not praying as much as should
why to prayer.
What to pray?

# 4
## Preachers Talk

Mary, Christine and Ian meet every three months to talk about their preaching. It's part of their responsibility as lay preachers and they take it seriously. This time Ian's flu has got in the way but Mary and Christine decide to meet anyway.

Christine asks Mary about how she prays and what she thinks prayer is all about.

Mary replies that she doesn't have much difficulty about prayer, except for prayers of intercession in public worship which they were trying to sort out anyway; nor, these days, too much difficulty about actually praying – not since she retired and a new central heating had been installed in her home.

Christine looks puzzled at the last point, so Mary explains. For her, she says, time and place are important in the way she prays. Retirement doesn't mean that she now has any more time than before, but that she does have a bit more freedom in organizing it. So after breakfast on every weekday she goes to her special room for twenty minutes or so.

Her special room?

The old box room, Alistair's tiny bedroom, is now her special room, used only for being quiet. It's her prayer room and reading room, nothing else. It's a very precious place, and that is where she prays, sitting in a comfy chair, having lit a candle and put on a CD.

What does she do?

She begins by reading the daily Bible reading from the lectionary in the Methodist Prayer Handbook; slowly, entering into it as deeply as she can, meditatively. If it's a story, she tries to become one of the characters, to imagine herself into the scene. That's something she learned from a speaker at a conference. That usually leads into deeper and deeper silence, focusing on something of God which has emerged in the reading. It's an alert silence, in which she is aware of herself and of the real life world, and also of God's presence. She hasn't really studied contemplative prayer, but she guesses that this is more or less what she is doing. She prefers to think of it as 'communing' with God, 'practising the presence of God'. Mostly she says very little, though sometimes she will repeat a verse of scripture, or a line of a hymn, over and over again, as the focus of her meditation. Mostly, she says, she just relaxes with God, listening to the silence of his presence and letting herself, people, places and situations be held in it.

How long has she been doing this?

She admits that she has only been praying like this since retirement and the new heating system, but it's not too different from what she has always done: made time for God and let him fill that time. She wasn't always as organized as she is now, but this is how she has tried to pray for many years. This was, in fact, how she became a preacher. Listening for God and to God in this way, she felt a call to preach. She didn't heard a voice, but she felt a growing conviction that preaching was something God wanted her to do, was calling her into. And that sort of thing happens often, she says. As she listens, she hears.

Mary explains that a key Bible verse for her is John 4.24, 'God is spirit, and those who worship him must worship in spirit and truth'. For her God is the Spirit which breathes through all creation, which animates all creatures, which is the giver and sustainer of all life. God is the Spirit which inspires music, art, poetry and every search for truth. God is the Spirit which disturbs all those people who seek for meaning and purpose in their lives. God is, she has come more recently to believe, the Spirit behind all religions.

Christine wants to pursue that but Mary hurries on.

God is Spirit – active, alive and working, she says, and prayer is being open to him. Look at how the Bible speaks of God, she says, all those busy and active words like creating, calling, equipping, sending, speaking, revealing. God does all that and people hear and see, they respond. That's how the Bible story unfolds. As the old hymn says, 'spirit to spirit thou dost speak'.

God is real, the reality behind or within everything we see, and prayer is tuning in to that divine reality.

Christine has not heard Mary talk quite like this before.

Mary then quotes the verse of Tennyson about God being 'closer than breathing, nearer than hands and feet'. She confesses that she doesn't know where ideas come from or where great music or new visions come from, but that she believes that they come from somewhere. They are 'inspired', she explains. She knows that the scientists are debating about how brains work and how minds relate to brains, but for her it is God the Spirit which Mozart tuned into and where visions and great ideas come from. She has, she says, no problem at all in believing that God affects human beings, that he 'works', that he 'does things', that 'Spirit' can speak to 'spirit'. And to prove that point she shares with Christine that experience she has had more than once of simply knowing that she must go and see someone, and finding when she got there that something had happened and she was needed to be there. 'If that's not God working, speaking, inspiring', she says, 'I don't know what is.' How it works she doesn't know. That it does happen, she is convinced.

'And Geoff s car parking space?', queries Christine.

'That's different,' Mary answers, 'quite different.'

*Questions for discussion*

1. Prayer has often been seen as a 'discipline', but Mary does not see it like that. What do you think of her idea of prayer as 'making time for God and letting him fill that time'?

2. Does Mary's picture of God ring bells with you? What are its strengths and weaknesses?

# 5
## June

June came to the next meeting of the House Group after a gap of several months. Her recent tragic bereavement was on everyone's mind, They had prayed, individually, in church and in the house group, for her daughter's recovery from cancer. June and her husband, Adrian, were loyal and faithful members of the church and everyone had been deeply concerned for them and for Julie, whom many of them had known since she was little. Julie, her family, June and Adrian had been surrounded by love, care and prayer. Friends from the church had taken Julie to several Healing Services. Some had helped, and some had hindered. But there had been no remission of the cancer. The minister had visited regularly, as had others from the church, and she had prayed and laid hands on Julie. But all to no avail. Julie had died, leaving behind a husband and two small daughters.

June knew what the group had been talking about in its last session, for Mary had told her. But once they started on the subject again, June amazed them. She told them that she had been embarrassed by many of the prayers she had heard prayed for Julie, and angry about some of them. Julie's cancer had been diagnosed as inoperable, and though she believed in both the mystery of life and faith and the marvels of God's love, she did not believe that God could do anything about her daughter's inoperable cancer. She spoke quietly, but she was determined to say what she thought needed to be said. When she had finished, there was a deep silence: not an embarrassed or an awkward silence, but a grateful one. June had spoken out of her pain with honesty, integrity and simplicity, and in the quietness the group recognized the special quality of what she had offered them.

Geoff recalled at first the sort of thing he had heard speakers say at some Healing Services: that Julie had not been healed because no one had believed that she could be healed. It was indeed what he would have said himself at one time. Now he didn't really think so. It just didn't ring true when you knew Adrian and June – Julie too – for they really were faithful, sincere and believing Christians. He couldn't understand why Julie had been struck down with cancer, or why so many prayers for healing had had no effect. But he wasn't any longer prepared to blame anyone for not having enough faith. This, he thought, must have been one of those times when God's answer to prayer had been 'No'.

The group let June talk about Julie and her illness for some time. She spoke about her initial shock, disbelief and anger. How she had shouted at God that it wasn't fair. She talked about the way she had clutched at straws when the oncologist had talked about drugs and treatments, or when she had heard cancer survivors talking on Women's Hour. She talked about bitterness and resentment giving way to resignation, resignation being replaced by grudging acceptance, then by peace and trust – sometimes all on the same day. She shared how she had been frightened and confused and how these moments came and went. She talked about her feelings of utter helplessness, of having to stand by, unable to do anything for Julie. She had done a lot for John and the grandchildren, of course, and there would be much to go on doing there, but that was somehow different. Now it was all over and, she said to the group, 'Life has to begin again', though inside she didn't really know how it could or would.

So she went on to talk about what people had said when they heard of Julie's illness and what she had thought about it. Almost the first question that she and nearly everybody else had asked was 'Why?' – Why should this happen to Julie? Why should this happen to anybody?

Why is there suffering at all? And she had listened to the answers and decided that none of them were right. No one said this to her face, of course, but she knew that some people

20

believed that suffering was the result of a person's sin. You got what you deserved. If you were bad, you suffered; if you were good, you prospered. She knew that there was some truth in this. Hadn't Granddad died of a heart attack at 53 when he was grossly overweight after a lifetime of puddings, cakes and sweets with no exercise at all? And wasn't he a heavy smoker too? Yes, lifestyle choice does come in there somewhere, June recognized that, But that's about as far as it goes, she had thought, as she listed all the rogues and rascals she had known who had died peacefully in great old age and all the good and nice people who had died tragically or young. No, that was no answer.

Nor could she accept that God sent, or allowed, suffering to test us or to make us better people. She had seen some people learn and grow through suffering, but in her long nursing career she had seen far more lives broken and faith lost by suffering. And Adrian's reaction had been that, if God allowed suffering to increase the total sum of human happiness and teach the human race lessons of care and compassion, then he'd got his calculations quite wrong. Others blamed evil, the Devil, cosmic powers bent on destroying God's creation and opposing his work. She had found that explanation tempting, but the minister had said that there was only one supreme God and that it was a heresy to think of two great competing powers of Good and Evil. Adrian had suggested that ministers were not always right.

She was in no doubt that human beings did cause quite a bit of suffering for their fellow human beings, sometimes deliberately, sometimes unintentionally, and she had reflected quite a lot about how much 'environmental factors' might have contributed to Julie's cancer

The more she had puzzled over these things, however, the more she had come to think that asking 'Why?' was not a very useful thing to do. Did there have to be a reason for Julie's illness? Why not think of it as 'just one of those things', just as

21

much a random occurrence as one of those road accidents where nobody is to blame at all? Bad things happen to people sometimes because they just happen to be in the wrong place at the wrong time. Just like that. 'Happenstance' was a lovely old word that seemed to do nicely. There was no reason for Julie's illness at all, she had concluded in the end. It was one of those awful facts of life. The better question to ask, she had come to think, was 'Where is God to be found in such chances and changes of life?'

At this point Mary decided to ask June what she had meant when she said that she had been embarrassed and angered by some of the prayers for Julie she had heard. June's first point surprised her. It was not one she had been expecting. June reminded Mary, as a preacher, of two common verses and responses used in the prayers of intercession in Sunday services. The first was 'Lord, in your mercy / Hear our prayer', and the second was 'The Lord hears our prayer / Thanks be to God'. June's objection to the first one was that it seemed to imply that God was at best a bit inattentive and at worst capricious and that therefore he needed to be persuaded to listen. Her God, she insisted, was simply not like that. Her objection to the second was that it did the very opposite. It took for granted that God would do what we asked, and that all would be well. And that, she said, was just not realistic.

Mary asked what June would prefer to say instead. What she looked for, June said, was a way of praying in public which allowed people to voice their concerns in ways which did not suggest either that God was indifferent or that a solution was immediately on the way. 'God did not need to be asked or reminded to love Julie', she said. 'His love was holding her all through her illness. And it didn't help us or the congregation to be told that all would be well when we all knew it couldn't be.' Mary thought that, as a preacher, she ought to think much more carefully about phrases that she used so easily and so often.

22

June's second point was about prayers that Julie would be healed when the diagnosis was that her illness was terminal. She felt that these prayers were unrealistic and that they made unfair demands on God. If healing didn't happen, and in Julie's case it hadn't happened, it was inevitable that people would start pointing the finger of blame, and that it would be pointed in one of two directions. There would be those who pointed it at Julie for not having enough faith, or something like that. And there would be those who pointed it at God for not answering prayer or for not delivering on his promises. June thought that was plainly unfair. It was one thing to blame God for something he could do something about, she said, but it wasn't fair to blame him for something he could do nothing about and, for her, inoperable cancer came into that category. 'You can't ask God to do the impossible', she said, 'though many people prayed for Julie as if you could and as if God did it every day. That kind of prayer creates unrealistic expectations', she added, 'and leads to nothing but disappointment and disillusionment when nothing actually happens.'

Finally, at Mary's prompting again, June talked a bit about the kind of prayers which had really helped her and Julie. She started by saying how helpful it was to know that they were all being remembered, week by week, in the prayers in church; and how good that felt, being 'remembered'. Then she said how helpful it had been to be told the same thing in the cards which came, though they often said little more than 'Thinking of you'. It was strange, she noted, how so many people in the church found it much easier to say that than to say that they were praying for you. And when people did pray for them, she said, it was the prayers which thanked God for being there and holding them all which helped the most; prayers which asked for nothing except that they might all know, whatever happened, that they were held in an eternal love; prayers which almost helped them to feel that underneath were the everlasting arms. That made them all smile a bit, for that was one of their minister's favourite phrases, and they had all played the 'How will she get it in this time?' game in her services.

Mary had never been to a Methodist Class Meeting like those held in chapels in her granny's day or so they said. But she felt that they had been in a Class Meeting tonight. That June had been giving her testimony, telling her story, sharing her faith. That God had been with them in a special way. That in listening to June's struggles, the group had been learning something important.

There was no way to end the evening except in silence.

## Questions for discussion

1. June doesn't agree with Geoff's theology that God is in control and God knows best. How would you sum up her understanding of things?

2. Prayers for the sick feature very often in intercessions in church. What do you expect to happen?

3. When things go wrong we say things like, 'It's just one of those things', and June uses the old word 'happenstance'. What are the implications for theology and for prayer if life really is like this?

# 6
## One Month Later

Andrew is playing with his trains again, and Mary has opened the House Group with prayer. She had a brainwave the previous weekend. For weeks the newspapers had been full of reports about the wettest autumn for years. Night after night the News on the telly had shown pictures of Worcester and York under many feet of water, railway lines washed away and disruption everywhere. Her own niece and nephew, who had only recently bought one of those little starter homes on a new estate, had come home from work a fortnight previously to find a foot of water in their lounge. 'Somebody bribed the planners to allow a housing estate to be built on a flood-plain', was Andrew's first reaction to the news. 'They should have known better than buy it in the first place', was his second. Mary worried about Andrew sometimes. He had never been very hot in the compassion department, but he was getting more like Victor Meldrew every year.

Last week's *Methodist Recorder* had been full of the same sort of pictures, together with stories of chapels and churches flooded out. But it was an item about a group of good Methodist folk from somewhere or another, it didn't really matter where, who had organized a prayer meeting for the rain to stop which had caught her attention. The *Recorder*, she discovered, seemed to suggest that this was a good example that others might follow. Her brainwave was to use this actual, real-life, current and pressing situation to explore the meaning of her chosen Bible passages for today. The fact that it tied in with what the Farming Vicar had been talking about on the radio was a bonus, and the clincher had come at the United Communion Service at St Ethelbertha's that Sunday night. They had used a set of intercessions from the new prayer book, Common Worship, and they had actually prayed 'for good weather and abundant harvests for all to share'. She wasn't sure she could believe what they were supposed to be saying, and

Christine's cough and splutter from two rows behind her had echoed round the church.

The House Group began by looking at the Lord's Prayer. Floods, they concluded, didn't have much connection with the first of the four requests it made to God, 'Thy kingdom come and thy will be done'. Yes, they agreed, when God's will was universally done and the world walked in his ways, which they took to be the sort of new world that the prayer was asking for, there wouldn't be the kind of floods they have in Bangladesh because the trees in the Himalayas are being cut down. But they didn't quite see that the flooding of the Severn or the Ouse came into the same category.

'Daily bread', yes, they understood how people who had been flooded out could cry out for help to cope. The question was: What sort of help could God be expected to provide, and how might he go about it? They had no doubt at all that people needed help in circumstances like that, and that, thank God, it was usually provided from many sources and in many ways. 'But', Christine asked, 'was that an answer to prayer?', and they weren't sure whether it was or wasn't. 'So why did you say "Thank God"?' was Christine's riposte.

They didn't stay long on the third request, the one asking for forgiveness. That didn't apply here, they agreed, unless you took Andrew's line about developers and planners. But did they know they needed forgiveness? And if they didn't, could they be forgiven anyway? They shelved that one.

That left, 'Lead us not into temptation and deliver us from evil', and what did that mean? Did it mean that the flooding was the work of the Devil? Was it asking God to stop the flooding? Could he, even if he wanted to? Or was it a request for help to stay calm and not get angry if you were flooded out? Or a plea that God would help you so that you weren't overwhelmed by despair? Or a not very subtle reminder that exaggerating your insurance claim was a morally dangerous thing to do? This was all good brainstorming stuff, they agreed, but it seemed to produce more questions than answers, even though most of the group said that the questions were 'very interesting'!

Mary then introduced another Bible verse which had long puzzled her. 'What about that famous saying of Jesus in Matthew 7.7–8 from the Sermon on the Mount', she asked them, 'the one which goes, "Ask and it will be given you; seek and you will find; knock, and the door will be opened for you. For everyone who asks receives, and everyone who seeks will find, and for everyone who knocks, the door will be opened"?'

At that Geoff gets in first. 'Look at that promise', he says, 'and listen to the one who makes it. Our Lord himself is speaking on behalf of our Heavenly Father. Our amazingly generous Heavenly Father just wants to do for us immeasurably more than we can ask or think, just as Paul testifies in Ephesians 3.20 and Jesus says many more times. Look what that verse says', he goes on, 'anything we ask in the name of Jesus we will receive.'

'So, that means that, if we ask for the rain to stop and the floods to go down they will?' queries Christine. 'Come on', she demands, 'we are supposed to be focused on the floods. So if we ask for the rain to stop, will we get what we ask for?' She doesn't give Geoff time to answer. 'Jesus also said that with only a mustard seed speck of faith we can command a mountain to be thrown into the sea and it will be done for us, didn't he? So why don't you do that then, have compassion on all the victims of these awful floods and make things better for them?'

'It doesn't mean that', Mary tries to say in her most conciliatory manner. 'These are just very powerful and vivid expressions, figures of speech. They aren't to be taken literally like that.' Geoff isn't sure that Mary is right, but he's glad of the break from Christine's attack.

'Hyperbole', says Vincent. 'You what?', three of the group say at once. 'Hyperbole, a figure of speech, the deliberate use

27

of exaggeration to make a point. I could eat a horse, that kind of thing', replies Vincent. 'Yes', says Mary, recovering her wits, 'a regular feature of Jewish teaching and storytelling, if I remember right. Camels and eyes of needles, taking the plank out of your own eye, that kind of thing. Right?', she asks, looking at Vincent. 'Right', he nods.

'What does it mean to ask for something in the name of Jesus?' asks Sarah, breaking the awkward silence. 'Because that's what we do at the end of most of our prayers isn't it? We end our prayers with "in the name of Jesus Christ our Lord", or something along those lines every time, don't we? "For the sake of Jesus Christ our Lord", is another one, isn't it? Is that the same?' It's Mary's turn to answer again, it seems. 'Yes, we do. And yes, it is. It means, firstly, that we are Christians who name the name of Jesus and are named with the name of Christ and our prayers, like everything else in our lives, are dedicated to his service. It means, secondly, that we want our prayers to be checked out to see if they are worthy things for followers of Jesus to be offering or to be asking for. It's another way of saying what Jesus himself said to the Father in his prayer in the Garden of Gethsemane, "Not my will but yours", not what I want but what you want, that kind of thing. It means, thirdly, that we are offering our feeble and inadequate prayers as part of something much bigger and better, the prayers of the whole church and of all the saints, and even the ongoing prayers of Jesus himself.' Three points. She'd preached on that one before!

But Geoff and Christine aren't happy. Geoff is prepared to admit to himself that he can't pray for God to stop the flooding, but he doesn't want to throw the baby out with the floodwater, as he thinks Mary is doing. Christine thinks Mary is not going far enough. Why can't you just admit that God can't do anything about the floods at all? she wants to ask, but she decides not to press it any more. Instead she asks what, if anything, Mary the preacher can pray about the flooding?

And Mary admits that she has problems here. She has few problems with the rest of the prayers in worship, she tells them, but the prayers of intercession, the prayers for other people and for the world in its pains and needs, do bother her. She has become increasingly uncomfortable with the intercessory prayers she hears in worship, almost to the point of not knowing what to say when she has to lead them. They all seem to be asking God for things – 'shopping list prayers', Andrew calls them. Should we be doing that, Mary wonders, treating God like a slot-machine dispensing answers to all our problems? And what happens when he doesn't deliver the goods? That's a recipe for anguish, as Mary knows from her own experience. And the worship books don't help here either. When a preacher says 'The Lord hears our prayer' and the reply comes 'Thanks be to God', she wonders, like June, if it's true and what difference it makes anyway? And when 'Lord, in your mercy' produces the response 'Hear our prayer', it sounds to her as if an appeal is being made to God's better nature to do something he'd rather not do. And as for, 'Lord, hear us' followed by 'Lord, graciously hear us', that just seems like the worst kind of grovelling. So, she says, she would use guided silence for her prayers for those caught up in the floods, holding these people and situations before God and asking God to bless them.

'Is that it?', thinks Geoff.

'What does that mean?', thinks Christine.

*Questions for discussion*

1. How would you pray if you had been flooded out? What would you pray for those who were being flooded?

2. The Gospels contain a number of sayings along the lines of 'ask and you will receive', e.g., Mark 11.24 (paralleled in Matthew 21.22), and John 14.13–14; 15.7 and 16.23–24. What do you make of them?

3. There are a few references to praying for others in worship in the New Testament, e.g., Philippians 1.9; Colossians 1.3 and 4.3; 1 Thessalonians 5.25 and 1 Timothy 2.1–3. What do you make of these?

4. Mary was unhappy with two of the most common versicles and responses used in prayers. Do you think she has a point? If so, can you suggest a versicle and response for prayers of intercession with which she might be happier?

# 7
## Leaning on a Gate

Mary is taking the dog for his midday walk and meets John strolling down the lane. It's one of those bright autumn afternoons when the mellowing colours are at their richest and there's still a bit of warmth in the sun. And it's not raining. They lean on a field gate. John talks. Mary listens.

'Felt a bit sorry for you last week, Mary. Got a bit flustered, didn't you. Mind you, I'm not surprised. Geoff and Christine go deep sometimes, don't they, and they don't listen to each other either. When old Granny Jenkins was trying to tell us something as kids, and we'd got our answers all ready before she'd finished, she'd look at us and ask us if we was listening or was we just waiting to speak. That's those two, if you ask me, always just waiting to speak. So don't let them get to you, as they say.

'I thought it was a good night. Getting down to a big question like that isn't easy, especially when there's such different answers. You remember Uncle Will and Uncle Jack, don't you? Preachers, both of them. Bachelor brothers, worked the same farm, and worked it well. Over there it was, where Manor Estate now is. Good farmers, never a cross word on what to do and when and how to do it. Not, though, when it came to religion.

'I remember they had two favourite texts. Uncle Jack's came from the Old Testament, 'Elijah's ravens, Will', he used to say, 'It's Elijah's ravens'. I remember after one particularly lively argument, Sam Mills, one of the lads who worked for them, painted two of them on the bonnet of Uncle Jack's tractor. Took months to wear off, they did. Would have got him the sack if he hadn't been so good with the pigs. Elijah's ravens? You don't know that one? And you a preacher too. Elijah the prophet was hiding in the wilderness, can't remember why, and God sends these ravens to feed him. The old Bible, of course. I know none of you young folk (that made Mary smile) use it any more. Pity. 'Elijah's ravens. God provides, Will. God provides', Uncle Jack would say.

'Uncle Will's text was another saying of Granny Jenkins, a wise old thing she was, that's where the uncles got it from. She used to say all kinds of things, but Uncle Will's favourite was: 'It ain't no good o' wishing and sitting down to wait; though God provides the fishing, you've got to dig the bait.' So he'd counter Uncle Jack's 'Elijah's ravens' with 'You've got to dig the bait, brother, dig the bait.' They could go on about that for hours, them two. Couldn't help thinking of them when Geoff and Christine were going on.

'Were you there the other week, when we had Harry Williams at chapel? Always like to hear a farmer in the pulpit. Do you remember what he said they had done out at Little Woodron, them and the Church? I can just about remember them doing that here, when this was still a village, before the town spread out. No? That Rogationtide service, going round the parish in the spring blessing the crops. Hadn't heard of that for years, but Harry said a lot of places were reviving it. Thought of that when you were talking about God blessing things.

'So I got my hymnbook out. No. The new one. I know I didn't like it at first, but I like it now. What I don't like is when we have that screen up and, well, they all sound the same to me and the words never fit the music. Don't start me on that. Looked up the Harvest hymns in the hymnbook. I thought they'd support Geoff a bit, praying for good weather and all that sort of thing. But they don't, you know. That lovely old Manx Fisherman's hymn we haven't sung for years, that one talks about God ruling the raging of the sea. "We Plough the Fields and Scatter" talks about God sending the snow in winter, the warmth to swell the grain, the breezes and the sunshine and soft refreshing rain. But them are the only two I can find that support old Uncle Jack's line. Most of them say how wonderful this world is, and praise the Maker for it, of course they do, but after that they seem to take Uncle Will's line. Even "We plough the Fields and Scatter", because if we didn't do that there wouldn't be any seeds or plants for God's warmth and rain to feed and water, would there? Like Granny Jenkins used to say,

> It ain't no good o' wishing and sitting down to wait;
> Though God provides the fishing, you've got to dig the bait.

That's the line the Harvest hymns take.

'I'm not quite sure, though, where that leaves us about praying for things and people, Mary. God loves us and wants only the best for us. That's the place to start, isn't it? So is prayer a way of helping that along? Of helping to make that happen for people? Obviously it works sometimes by reminding us of things we must do. If you pray for the starving in Africa; it reminds me in the pew to put my name on the House-to-House Collection list in Christian Aid Week. Right? Right. But maybe there is more to it than that, like you said? Maybe prayer is us sort of adding our bit to God's to help things on in ways we don't understand? Our thoughts, our goodwill, our compassion, that kind of thing? Don't know. Just wondering.

'We'd better get on. Dog's had his rest and he's ready for off again.'

*Questions for discussion*

1. Uncle Jack and Uncle Will are discussing the idea of 'providence'. What, if anything, does that word mean to you?

2. The uncles agree that God 'provides'. They differ in saying how. How would you say that 'God provides'?

3. In what ways is 'Helping God's love along' a helpful way of thinking about prayer?

# 8
## On the Common Again

A few days later Vincent is on the Common again with his dog. Geoff doesn't have a dog, but he is making one of his periodic and usually short-lived attempts at taking up jogging. When he sees Vincent, he is glad of the excuse to stop. The conversation comes round to prayer.

'You don't have any problems with prayer, then, Geoff?'

'I didn't say that. I don't pray as often as I think I should, or even as often as I want to. I have dry times when God doesn't feel very close and it's hard to pray. And I sometimes get angry with God about the answers I get when I'm praying for people.'

'But you do believe that God answers prayer?'

'Yes. Always, As somebody said, "More things are wrought by prayer than this world dreams of".'

'Tennyson.'

'Oh, thanks. What about, "Thou art coming to a king, large petitions with thee bring"?'

'Don't know that one, Geoff.'

'Old Methodist hymn, Vincent.'

'Well, I wouldn't know that then, would I?'

'Suppose not. What about, "He is ever more ready to hear than we are to pray"?'

'Bible? No. It's a collect, I think, but not sure which. Doesn't matter, but you do believe that God answers prayer?.'

'Yes. Always. But only when prayer is offered "in the name of Jesus".'

'Yes, we talked about that didn't we? What do you think it means to say that?'

'It means that there are all kinds of things that we shouldn't ask God for in prayer. We shouldn't ask him to let us win the Lottery. We shouldn't ask him to spoil the film when we've been flashed by a speed camera. We shouldn't ask him – to give you an example from my own line of business – to make us win that contract we've tendered for. We shouldn't ask for those things because Jesus wouldn't ask for them. If you'd be ashamed or embarrassed to ask for something in the presence of Jesus, then that's the sort of request which you shouldn't be making anyway and which God won't grant if you do.'

'Okay. There's a proper sort of thing to pray for, honest, loving, unselfish and all that. Does God answer every time?'

'Yes'.

'Yes?'

'Yes. But the answer isn't always 'Yes'. Sometimes it is. Sometimes it's 'No'. Sometimes it's 'Wait'. Sometimes it's 'Yes' but in ways you never imagined. Sometimes it's 'Yes' but in ways you can't actually see at the time or for a long time after. And sometimes what looks like a 'No' turns out to be a 'Yes'. But there is always an answer. Because that's what Jesus promises us: "Whatever you ask in my name, I will do it."'

'Even when you ask for a car parking space, Geoff?'

'Yes, even then, because God loves his children and delights to meet their needs, and finding a car parking space is a real need.'

'But it's a bit on the trivial side, isn't it?'

'Maybe, maybe not.'

'It's certainly a bit on the selfish, just-for-me side, though, isn't it, like a smaller version of wanting to win the lottery?'

'No it isn't. It is personal and it is small scale. I grant you both of those descriptions. But it's a real, genuine need. And God wants to meet that sort of need for us, even in the details.'

'So there's no such thing as "unanswered prayer"?'

'Not if it's a proper prayer in the first place, no. Though we don't always like the answers. But God knows best. And he is in control. Believe me.

'Better go on. Bye now.'

'Bye.'

*Questions for discussion*

1. What do you think of Geoff's picture of God? What are its strengths and weaknesses?

2. Geoff insists that 'Yes', 'No', or 'Wait' are God's answers to prayer. What do you think?

3. Praying for a car parking space is obviously an emotive issue. How do you react to the idea?

# 9
## Sue Talks to the Minister

Although Sue had not enjoyed the last few House Groups, she had found the way June shared herself with them all deeply moving. She had come home that night much richer, she felt, than she had gone out. She also felt that some light was beginning to dawn on this whole business of prayer, and she was glad when the minister rang to arrange a pastoral visit. Now, having shared each other's news, sorted out a couple of church jobs, and reviewed everything that the Farming Vicar's broadcast had set in motion, they were drinking coffee, and Sue wasn't quite sure what to talk about next.

'So', said Clare, to help her along a bit, 'have I got this right? You were taken aback by that broadcast in which the Farming Vicar seemed to suggest that God couldn't really change things or help with things?' Sue nodded. 'But when June talked about what had happened to her and her family and expressed her conviction that God had been with them through all their sufferings, that rang bells for you?' Sue nodded again, 'You felt that, although God hadn't been able to do anything to save Julie, nevertheless he had been there with them and for them in that awful crisis?' Sue nodded. 'So, what sort of God do you believe in, Sue?' asked Clare, as she sat back and waited for an answer.

Sue stuttered a bit at first but eventually began to reply. 'I believe in a loving God', she said, 'a God who cares for everything and everybody; a good God who made the world and who loves all that he has made.' It was Clare's turn to nod. 'I believe this', Sue went on, 'because of Jesus, who was "God with us", who came to share our life and show us God's love.'

Clare nodded again, before asking, 'And what pictures of this loving God do you have in your mind when you pray or think about him?'

Sue stuttered again. '"Father"', she said, 'must be one. "King" is another, though that makes him aloof and distant sometimes. "Friend", especially when I think about Jesus. Things like that.' Clare nodded. 'But', Sue went on, 'sometimes I don't have any pictures at all, I think that God is just there, like air, or like water must be for fish.'

'"The one in whom we live and move and have our being"', Clare added, and then remembered that she shouldn't interrupt. Fortunately, Sue didn't look blank. 'Yes', she said, 'that's it, something like that. But . . . ' She paused, smiling.

'But . . . ?', prompted Clare.

'But, what about all that stuff about God doing things, saving people, appearing to Moses, dividing the Red Sea, making the Israelites a great nation and punishing their enemies, calling people to be prophets, making Mary pregnant, saving people, bringing Jesus back from the dead, giving the Holy Spirit – doing all the kinds of things that we list in the Communion Service?'

'You mean "the mighty acts of God".'

'Do I? I don't know.'

'You mean, "a God who acts", who does things, who intervenes to do good in his world?'

'I suppose I do, and it's that God that the Farming Vicar didn't seem to believe in, and I'm just not sure. Haven't we gone round in a circle again?'

There was an uncomfortable silence which seemed to Sue to last quite a long time. 'Do you believe in that sort of God, Clare?', she asked.

Although Clare believed in honesty of preaching, this felt a bit too much like being put on the spot. But an honest question needed an honest answer. 'No', she said, 'I don't. I believe in a "one in whom we live and move and have our being" sort of God, whose love is the energy of life itself, whose power and love sustains all life. That's the sort of God I believe in. A God who works in and through nature, and in and through people.'

Sue was quiet. Then she said, 'That's June's sort of God, isn't it? And that's why you keep going on about that Bible verse

38

about, "The Eternal God is our dwelling place, and underneath are the everlasting arms", isn't it?'

'I suppose it is', said a slightly surprised Clare, who had to go to see about a funeral.

But they didn't part until they had agreed another time for Clare to call back.

*Questions for discussion*

1. What is your favourite picture of God?

2. 'The God who acts' used to be a popular way of describing the Christian God, but has now slipped from favour. Why do you think that this has happened?

3. 'The one in whom we live and move and have our being.' In what ways do you find this a helpful, or unhelpful, way of speaking about God?

# 10
## The Minister Talks to Sue

In Sue's kitchen a week later, over more coffee, Sue asked Clare directly, 'How do you pray to your God?'

'Much of the time', Clare replied, 'I'm happy to use the same kind of images of God that you said you used. When I pray I call God "Father", sometimes even – but not very often in public – "Mother", or "Lord God", or at times "Lord God our Heavenly Father". I don't often address God as "Heavenly King", though, and I'm very cagey about "Almighty God".'

Sue chipped in that she remembered a bit of the sermon on that one.

Clare continued, 'I like to use a variety of different words when I address God, though I admit to falling back on one or two basic ones when my imagination dries up. So I suppose my standard ones are "Eternal God", "God of Grace and God of Glory" and "God of Life and Light and Love". Actually, I've found the Collects in the new Methodist Worship Book very helpful, for they use a lot of new and imaginative ways of addressing God. And when you compare them with the Collects in the new Anglican Common Worship book, you see how good they really are. As I said to Father Tony – and he agreed – the Anglican collects are still stuck in the old "Almighty God" rut.

After finishing a mouthful of biscuit, Clare got back to the point: 'But it's more than just changing the way you address God, though that's important. It's also what you think you are really doing. If you think of God as a person – Father, Lord, King: that kind of picture – then prayer is like talking to someone. If that someone is a good listener, you can tell them anything and everything. If that someone knows you and loves you, they listen and respond. If you need something from that someone, you ask, and how you ask depends on who they are and what you want; and they might want to give it to you, or they might not. Asking a Traffic Warden not to give you a ticket is a bit different from asking you for another cup of coffee. Yes, please. Thanks. So if you think of God in terms of those pictures – Father, Lord, King and so on – prayer is about talking to God, often with a heavy asking component: asking for forgiveness, or asking for help for yourself or for others. And that brings you into the difficult area of requests which, apparently, are not answered.

'I don't myself find this approach very helpful. But it is, I believe, the way that most people have been taught to think of God and to pray to him, and the way that they still follow. So if I'm unhappy with it, how do I pray? One of my favourite ways of thinking about God, as I think I mentioned last week, is as "the one in whom we live and move and have our being". That's a way of thinking about God, coming from some ancient Greek philosopher, which Paul quotes with approval when he's preaching to the Greeks in Athens. [The reference is to Acts 17.28, but Clare can't remember chapters and verses]. In other words, I think of God as the love which is the energy of life itself, and that basic idea is not very different from what you said about air to us and water to fish. You've noticed that one of my favourite Bible verses is "The Eternal God is our dwelling place, and underneath are the everlasting arms" [Deuteronomy 33:27], which expresses the same conviction. It's a bit of a shock to discover a different translation in the new versions of the Bible, But that won't stop me using the more familiar words!'

Clare really ought to watch her biscuit intake, thought Sue.

'So, praying to a God like this is different from having a conversation with a person or asking someone for something. Must be. So there's a lot of silence sometimes. Or poetry, or pictures, or music. It's a sort of meditation, I suppose, which takes you out of yourself and into something bigger. It's like tuning in to a symphony on the radio, losing yourself in it, but becoming very, very aware of things. "Focusing" is another word for it, becoming absorbed in something, caught up in it.'

Sue nodded. She could understand this sort of prayer. She used it herself sometimes.

'So praying for other people when you think of God in this way', continued Clare, 'means holding people or places or situations in your mind in the conscious presence of God, offering your concern for them or anxiety about them, adding the energy of your love to the energy of God's love. That kind of thing. It also means that, by entering imaginatively into someone else's situation, you yourself are changed. Often, too often, I finish praying like that knowing there is something I must do. And that's not easy. Did I say last week that the God I believe in is a God who works in and through nature, and in and through people? Thought I did. And that's how he does it, by changing me and you, and by drawing our loving concern into his life-giving energy of love which sustains all things.'

Sue didn't look entirely convinced.

'Okay then, here are two old ways of putting this and a new one. Have you heard of Theresa of Avila, sixteenth century, Spanish nun and mystic? Well, she said this:

> Christ has no body now on earth but yours;
>   no hands but yours, no feet but yours.
> Yours are the eyes through which must look out
>   Christ's compassion on the world.
> Yours are the feet with which He is to go about doing good.
> Yours are the hands with which He is to bless men now.

Take out the word 'Christ' and put in the word 'God' and you're getting there. Then do the same with the old Sunday School ditty:

> Christ has no hands but our hands to do his work today,
> He has no lives but our lives to win men for his way;
> He has no lips but our lips to tell men how he died,
> He has no feet but our feet to lead them to his side.

42

The new one is this lovely song from Nicaragua:

> Sent by the Lord am I,
> my hands are ready now
> to make the earth the place
> in which the kingdom comes.
>
> The angels cannot change
> a world of hurt and pain
> into a world of love,
> of justice and of peace.
> The task is mine to do,
> to set it really free.
> O, help me to obey,
> help me to do your will.

Does that help? Then there's this saying, which oversimplifies all kinds of things, but there's something in it: "Prayer doesn't change things. Prayer changes people, and people change things." That's how it seems to me.'

*Questions for discussion*

1. If you had to compose the first prayer for use in church next Sunday morning, how would you address God?

2. God as a Person or as the Energy which drives the universe. Are these alternatives? Do we have to choose?

3. What do you find helpful in the saying of St Theresa of Avila, the Sunday School chorus and the worship song from Nicaragua about prayers of intercession? What are their weaknesses?

# 11
## The Ministers' Fellowship

Later that week there was a lively discussion at the monthly Ministers' Fellowship in the town. It was prompted by Clare telling the seven ministers present about her conversation with Sue – without, of course, mentioning any names – and about the discussions which had been going on in her church.

She indicated how pleased she was that her folk were talking about something other than vandalism and money-raising. The other ministers were envious. They asked what had started the discussions. 'Interesting', they said. They asked about the House Group. 'Impressive', they said. They asked what Clare herself had said. 'Impossible', one of them said. A time of thoughtful sharing followed!

Clare spent the next ten minutes defending herself. Having pointed out that believing that God was the 'one in whom we live and move and have our being' was not heretical – though none of them had suggested it was – she threw in a reference to God as the 'Ground of our Being' from some modern theologian whose name she couldn't remember. She did, however, remember Paul's marvellous description of God at the end of Romans 11 as 'Source, Guide and Goal of all that is', but then had to counter those whose Bibles were a bit more up to date than the New English. She was tempted to quote 'Being's source begins to be' from one of her favourite Christmas hymns and the first verse of 'Being of beings, God of love' but thought that Wesley's hymns would be lost on her ecumenical friends. Her Old Testament verse (Deuteronomy 33.27) was very well received. Thinking of God like this did not reduce him to some sort of impersonal force, she concluded, just as thinking of God as a person didn't identify him as an old man in the sky with a white beard.

She was not alone in her approach. Several colleagues contributed similar views. On the specific question of prayers of intercession, the other Methodist there chipped in with what he described as the most helpful thing he'd ever read about prayers of intercession. It came, he said, from a 'classic' book from the 1960s which suggested that our prayers of intercession are the way we offer our love, concern and energy to God to help him do his work. 'God', he said, 'needs our prayers and invites them as a way of helping him.' Clare thought that this was a picture of God that made sense.

There were those there who saw nothing wrong with thinking of God in very traditional terms as Father, Lord and King, and everything right with thinking of him as Almighty. 'If God is not almighty, then he's not God', one colleague insisted. We pray to him, others said, because he tells us to. Even though God knows our needs before we ask, they added, praying is a way of acknowledging our dependence on him and avoiding taking things for granted – something which, they all said, was very easy to do. It's a way, they insisted, of recognizing our need of God and of showing our gratitude.

Their response to the riddle of 'unanswered' prayer was similar to Geoff's. Prayer is always answered. The answer might be 'Yes', 'No' or 'Wait', but an answer is always given because God is in control and is working his purposes out, despite all the forces of evil and death which are trying hard to prevent his goals being achieved. 'At this stage', one said, 'we can't see enough to recognize how all his answers to our prayer fit into that process. But they do. It may sometimes be very hard to believe, but that's the way it is.' One day, they said, when the process is completed, we will be able to look back and see God's hand in everything and thank him for it.

One minister sat silent, listening to both points of view but saying nothing. Eventually the others asked him what he thought, where he stood on this issue. He said that he didn't find either of their ways of looking at things very helpful, even though they were based on centuries of serious thought and experience. Both of them assumed that God was 'real', either as a real 'person' or as a real 'force' behind or within the

45

universe, and he couldn't go along with that.

They pressed him about what he could go along with, about what, if anything, he did believe. They didn't call him an atheist who ought to look for another job, though a glance between two of them suggested that's what they might have been thinking. For this was a minister they knew and respected, whose leading of worship was rich and real, whose care for people and commitment to justice and peace was practical and whom they knew to be a person of prayer. So they listened as he explained that, for him, the word 'God' didn't refer to a heavenly being or a life-giving power. It didn't, in fact, refer to any 'thing' at all. He used the word 'God', therefore, in relation to making sense of life, creating meaning when so much around us is meaningless. For him 'faith' was making a decision to live by certain values – those seen clearest of all in Jesus – and to resist the influence of those who saw life in terms of getting, having and keeping. It was to live 'as if': as if humanity matters, as if the Bible story-world expresses truth, as if love is at the heart of things, as if the world did not just happen but was created – as if all those convictions were worth living for, and dying for. 'That's what I mean when I say "I believe in God"', he said. 'The word "God" is shorthand for all of that.'

When they asked him about prayer, he answered that for him prayer was meditation and music and poetry and quiet and reading the paper and getting angry at the way things so often are, and laughter and tears. Above all, he said, quoting Paul from Philippians 4.8, prayer was about filling your thoughts with those things which are true, noble, just, pure, loveable, attractive, excellent and admirable and, by so doing, being uplifted and encouraged to contribute more of them to a desperately needy world.

They didn't come to any agreed conclusion on that morning.

But, as they always did, they prayed together, reflecting on the amazing grace and the gleaming glory of God, acknowledging failure and need, receiving encouragement and renewal, upholding each other and others in their need and going out in peace to love and serve God and his world in the name of Jesus.

*Questions for discussion*

1. Though Deuteronomy 33.27 was 'very well received' by the ministers, it is a problematic text. Is it important that Clare's approach to prayer can claim better biblical support? If not, why not? If so, try to offer some suggestions.

2. In what ways is our overall understanding of God affected by the idea that he needs our prayers to help him?

3. What do you make of the anonymous minister with the unusual views?

# Part 2

# Thinking Through The Issues

# 12
## What is Prayer?

Sue's question over coffee started a chain of discussions, conversations and reflections on prayer among the folk associated with Trepolpen United Church. As a result, we have encountered a wide variety of views about prayer and about how it 'works' or doesn't 'work'. We now turn to look at the issues raised in a rather more systematic way.

There is no religion, ancient or modern, in which prayer – public or private, corporate or individual – does not feature. It is no surprise, therefore, that of the 1,121 prayers found in the *Oxford Book of Prayer*, 271 come from sources other than the Bible and from traditions other than Christianity. One tradition of faith not represented is New Age spirituality, perhaps because it only arrived on the scene after the book was published. In Britain today, however, the incense sticks and crystals of New Age, the call to prayer sounding from the mosque, the Buddhist prayer wheel, and the mantras chanted by the monks of Hare Krishna are familiar features of religion.

Moreover, if questionnaires and surveys are to be believed, many more people in our nominally Christian country pray than ever demonstrate any allegiance to the Christian faith by actually going to church. What exactly so many do and why they do it would make a fascinating topic for research, but it is worth underlining that they claim to pray.

Prayer, then, doubtless means different things to the people who practise it in the many different religions found in the UK today. In the rest of this book, however, we will confine our thinking to Christian prayer. Even here, of course, a vast range of styles can be discerned but, to simplify our discussion, we will divide Christian prayer into two types. 'public' (or corporate) prayer and 'private' (or individual) prayer.

*Public Prayer*

A good example of one style of 'public' prayer is that found in
the daily services of Morning or Evening Prayer which are said
in our cathedrals and can sometimes still be found in parish
churches. Here a service of prayers and Bible readings is 'said'
or, occasionally on Sundays and special days, 'sung' from a
Prayer Book. The predominant voice is that of the priest who
reads the set prayers. The congregation joins in the Lord's
Prayer, says the responses to one-sentence prayers led by the
priest and adds its old Hebrew 'Amen' ('Yes', 'Agreed', 'So be
it') at the end. In the prayers of this service the standard
elements of public prayer are all present: adoration or praise,
confession, thanksgiving, intercession, blessing and dedication.
It is this service, refocused on a sermon and with the addition
of congregational hymns, which forms the usual Sunday
Service of most Methodist and United Reformed churches
today.

A very different but equally good example of 'public' prayer
is the prayer offered in times of 'worship' and 'ministry' in
churches which have been influenced by the charismatic
movement. There a Worship Leader takes responsibility for
these different times of prayer, but the prayers themselves are
offered, unscripted and unplanned, from all parts of the
building by many different individuals. Usually, but not
always, these prayers are short, especially in the 'ministry'
prayer time when the prayers may consist of no more than
naming a person or specifying a situation. But the church
is not silent. Even those not praying aloud for the congregation
to hear will be praying in a quiet but audible voice. And
others will be adding their own vocal 'Amen' or 'Yes,
Lord' or other expressions by which they identify with the
prayers being said. In those churches which practise 'speaking
in tongues' not all the prayers are in English; and in those
churches with a music group, there may well be, especially in

the 'worship' prayer time, background singing or instrumental music.

Different again are services of prayer like the Vigil or the Taizé service. A Taizé service will feature much quiet singing of Taizé chants as well as Bible readings and silence, and the mix in each service will vary. Through the repetition of the chants, some of which are in Latin, the singers expect to move through the singing and the words into the silence of God's peaceful presence. The building will usually be darkened, probably with a single candle as a focus, and the congregation will often be seated on the floor in a circle. Vigils come in many forms, but usually they centre on an issue about which people have come together to pray. The prayers may be spoken or silent, but an increasingly common feature is the lighting of candles. Members of the congregation are invited to express their prayer and concern by lighting a candle and placing it on or near the focal point of the vigil. Variations include placing a stone or card or shell, whatever it is that they have been given on entering the building, at the focal point. Here prayer is expressed in action and gesture, often without words.

The classic book referred to in the discussion at the Ministers' Fellowship is J. Neville Ward's *The Use of Praying* (Epworth Press 1967, reprinted frequently and still in print). In it Ward repeatedly makes the point that it is in the Eucharist that we see most clearly what prayer in the Christian tradition really is, and that it begins and ends in thanking and offering. For him the Eucharist is in fact Christian prayer in its fullness. It is 'the central and representative act of Christian prayer' and, in dealing with the different elements of prayer, he draws attention to the forms that they take in the Eucharist. Although not all Christians would share Ward's devotion to the Eucharist or even be comfortable in using the word, we can include this sacrament as another example of public prayer, thanks to its overall character and detailed structure.

*Private Prayer*

Ward also insists that, for the Christian, corporate prayer is primary and private prayer is secondary. This does not mean, he adds, that private prayer is 'expendable'. Because it is so varied, however, it is much more difficult to describe. Perhaps the model of private prayer which many still think is expected of them is a private version of Morning or Evening Prayer in which the Bible is read and prayers are said in a 'Quiet Time'. The two orders of Prayer in the Morning and Prayer in the Evening provided in *Common Worship* and in *The Methodist Worship Book* or the prayers for each day of the month in the annual *Methodist Prayer Handbook* are useful resources for those who find this approach helpful.

Mary's method of using time in her special room is very similar, but it's clear that many can't and don't pray in this way. Vincent, for example, only manages two quick *Hail Marys* before he goes to sleep but will 'just sit' in the cathedral every time he's in town. Sarah, who feels bad about what she doesn't do, has her favourite bench on the Common. How do other people actually pray? Some talk to God over the washing up or as they walk the dog or mow the lawn. Some do yoga or meditation. Some use 'arrow prayers', brief moments of focused concern. Some burn incense sticks and put on a CD. Some buy books of prayers, read poetry, or meditate on hymns. Some join in the daily prayers on the radio, or put on a tape in the car on the way to work. Some use none of these methods, but commit themselves to a practical task as their way of 'thanking and offering'.

There are, it seems, a great many ways in which Christian people in Britain 'practise the presence of God', and I offer you that phrase as a good description or definition of prayer. It is based on the title of a collection of the letters and sayings of Brother Lawrence (Nicholas Herman), a Frenchman who was born around 1611, entered the Carmelite monastery in Paris in 1649 as a lay brother and worked in the monastery kitchen until his blindness made this impossible. He died in 1691. For another definition of prayer I suggest this:

> Prayer is the communication and communion, spoken and unspoken, that takes place between ourselves and God (in whatever terms we think of the Power behind the universe).

From our glance at the forms which this communication can take, we see that it can be public or private, formal or informal, corporate or individual, with words or without words, momentary or sustained, and that it involves both listening to God and speaking to God.

Whenever you begin to talk or read about prayer, however, one thing is abundantly clear, namely, that there is much guilt around the business of private prayer. For many find it to be a burden rather than a delight; and many more are 'oppressed by things undone' and very conscious of the gap between what they do and what they think they ought to do in the prayer department. Such people need to hear Vincent's parting words to Sarah at the end of chapter 3.

It may help also to reflect that each of the following is a prayer:

> God, help me to pray
> God, help me to want to pray
> God, help me to want to want to pray.

*Questions for discussion*

1. 'Pray as you can, not as you can't.' Is this a dictum you have followed? If so, how? If not, why not?

2. What do you think about the fact that *The Oxford Book of Prayer* includes prayers from other traditions of faith?

3. 'Prayer is communication and communion with God.' Does that say enough for a working definition of prayer, or would you say more?

# 13
# The Dynamics of Prayer

Prayer is the soul's sincere desire,
Uttered or unexpressed,
The motion of a hidden fire
That trembles in the breast

Whatever else prayer may be, this first verse of James Montgomery's old hymn shows that it is an expression of emotion and feeling, sometimes inarticulate, sometimes put into words. Neville Ward, as we have seen, roots the beginning and end of prayer in 'thanking' and 'offering'. But for the really raw emotions at the heart of prayer we need to look at the psalms in the Old Testament, which over the years have influenced the public and private prayers of a great many people.

Judaism and Christianity agree on the belief that God exists, that there is a Supreme Being, an Ultimate Reality, a Power behind the Universe. They both say, moreover, that we should speak of this Supreme Being, Ultimate Reality and Power behind the Universe in personal rather than impersonal ways, that we should use the word 'he' rather than 'it' when we speak of 'God'. They both assert, finally, that the word which comes closest to indicating what God is like is 'love', but that, because God is beyond our understanding, imagining and describing, every word we may want to use to speak about him must be clothed in invisible inverted commas.

Given this belief, Jews and Christians – and others too, of course, whose names for God are different – have a focus for voicing how they feel, someone to whom they can express their joy or agony, someone with whom to laugh or to cry. There is, they affirm – and, granted the minuteness of our overcrowded planet and the vastness of the universe, this is a truly amazing claim – a God who is interested in them and concerned about them. The Victorian children's hymn puts it with a naïve but accurate boldness,

> God who made the earth,
> The air, the sky, the sea,
> Who gave the light its birth,
> Careth for me.

Granted the history of the 'bloody twentieth century', however, most of us will have had experiences which make that very hard indeed to believe. Nevertheless it is the basic affirmation of our Christian tradition. So prayer, to go back to our definition, is communication and communion with a concerned and interested God to whom we matter a great deal.

The majority of the psalms fall into one of two categories – 'praise' or 'lament' – and these are the terms I prefer to use to describe the basic dynamics of prayer rather than Ward's 'thanking' and 'offering'.

*Praise*

> O enter then His gates with praise;
> Approach with joy His courts unto;
> Praise, laud, and bless His name always,
> For it is seemly so to do.

This is the third verse of William Kethe's translation of Psalm 1 in the hymn, 'All people that on earth do dwell'. It can stand as a heading as we look at the dynamic of 'praise'.

Psalms of praise give voice to a joyful 'Yes', often an against-the-odds 'Yes', shouted sometimes by the whole community gathered in worship and on other occasions by individual worshippers. They are songs of celebration. They affirm life and receive it gratefully as a gift. It is as if the worship leader calls the people to worship with, 'Isn't it great to be alive!' and the choirs and congregation reply, 'Indeed it is!' – 'It is! It is!' – 'Amen! Amen!' What evokes this outpouring of emotion, which takes the form of grateful praise and thanksgiving to God, varies from psalm to psalm.

Psalm 103 is a good example. In verses 2–5 the psalmist counts the many blessings he has received from God. God has forgiven his sin, healed his diseases, saved him from the Pit, crowned him with love, satisfied him with good things, and renewed his youth. Other psalms repeat the list. God has lifted the psalmist out of the 'miry bog' of illness (Psalm 40), saved him from untimely death (Psalm 30), brought victory in war (Psalm 18), heard and answered prayer (Psalms 66 and 116), destroyed the wicked (Psalms 73 and 75) and made the fields and farms prosper (Psalm 67).

We may or may not find this a helpful way of speaking, for it raises all the questions about how God can be said to act in our world. After a century, for example, in which unchecked human wickedness resulted in genocidal terror can we claim that God destroys the wicked? And why are his 'blessings' so unequally distributed (plenty for the few and famine or poverty for the many) and so arbitrarily bestowed (why was the psalmist saved from untimely death but not June's daughter?). These are hard questions and they must be addressed. However, they should not blind us, at this point, to the sense of gratitude which throbs through the psalms of praise. These psalms do not take things for granted. They look out at life and say 'Thank You' for its gifts and giftedness. They express simple gratitude, and that's no bad thing in any time and place.

Gratitude, however is only one of the emotions which give rise to psalms of praise. In the rest of Psalm 103 the psalmist is moved to praise by reflecting on what God is like. God has made himself known as Israel's God and Saviour, calling his people into being, delivering them from oppression and blessing them with his guidance (verses 6–7). He has shown in his own special way the qualities associated with human fatherhood at its best – compassion, care and understanding; he is 'merciful and gracious, slow to anger and abounding in steadfast love' (verses 8–18).

This passage repeats the description of God from Exodus 34.6–7, echoes of which are found in most parts of the Old Testament. The psalmist testifies to Israel's continuing experience of what this 'core credo' affirms, speaking of God's 'amazing grace', his forgiving and renewing generosity and his dependable kindness. He declares, indeed, that he himself feels embraced by this 'new every morning' kind of love, a love which will not let him go, which has taken his sins and mistakes and put them behind him. So he is amazed by grace, moved to joy, love and worship in the depth of his being because of the love of God. This is another common feature of the psalms of praise.

There is more. In verses 19–22 the psalmist catches a glimpse of the worship of the LORD, the King of Heaven. Worshipping in the temple, he finds himself caught up into the very worship of heaven itself, with his voice added to those of 'angels, archangels and all the company of heaven'. Experiences like this are not common in the Bible, nor do they happen very often in our lives today, but, when they do occur, they put us in touch with something higher, deeper, and richer, and provide another way in which the response of 'praise' is generated in us.

Perhaps it is Psalm 8 which best expresses this experience of wonder. We may look at a night sky, a sunrise, or a view. We may see a new baby, or be present at a sublime moment of human achievement. Such experiences make us whisper a 'Wow' that melts into silence. That too is praise.

All this is summed up in Joseph Addison's hymn of 1712:

> When all thy mercies, O my God,
>   My rising soul surveys,
> Transported with the view, I'm lost
>   In wonder, love and praise.

*Lament*

> Out of the depths I cry to thee,
> Lord God! O hear my prayer!
> Incline a gracious ear to me,
> And bid me not despair.

This verse from Martin Luther's powerful version of Psalm 130 contains two words – 'depths' and 'despair' - not listed in dictionary definitions of prayer. Add to them the word 'anger' and you have the basic ingredients of the psalms of lament, the other main category into which the psalms can be divided.

Psalm 130 is, in fact, quite mild as laments go. Psalm 74 is much more full-blooded. The New Jerusalem Bible entitles it 'Lament on the sack of the Temple', and that may well be right. It hurls urgent questions at God: Why has this happened? (twice each in verses 1 and 11); and How long will it be before God does anything about it? (verse 10). It complains that God is dragging his feet and demands that he acts. He must 'remember!' (verses 2, 18, and 22), 'not forget!' (verses 19 and 23), 'come and see' (verse 3), 'save his people' (verse 19), 'honour his covenant' (verse 20), and 'not let the downtrodden be shamed' (verse 2 1). He must do something! (verse 22). Time and again God is reminded in no uncertain terms that his reputation is at stake when his people suffer. He is the one being insulted by his enemies! The psalmist appeals shamelessly to God's past deeds – you have done it before, so do it again! And God is blamed directly for this trouble. His people have not brought all this upon themselves. It is not their fault, It is his! And the psalmist demands an answer. This is an angry psalm of accusation, and the accused is God.

Just as the psalms of praise give voice to a joyful 'Yes', the psalms of lament voice a powerful 'No'. They are cries of pain, shouted angrily by people of faith gathered in worship or, on other occasions, wrung out of the depths of an anguished individual's despair. They emerge from desperate situations where the only realities seem to be evil, darkness and death. They are cries of distress, acts of defiance, and pleas for help.

Thus in the psalms, the oldest resources for spirituality and liturgy available to us in our tradition of faith, we have extremely diverse material: expressions of gratitude for life's blessings and cries of anguish in its troubles. Prayer arises, it seems, out of a deep human need to voice our feelings in both sets of circumstances.

The basic dynamic of prayer, then, is our human need – individual and corporate – to give expression to our joy or our pain. In articulating these basic emotions we do not rejoice or cry into a void. We direct our praise or our lament to God, for we believe that we are not alone in the universe.

## *Questions for discussion*

1. In the light of this discussion, what do you think lies at the heart of prayer?

2. The lament type of prayer does not feature very much in our corporate prayers today. How, then, can we deal with our strong feelings of hurt, anger, and frustration?

3. Have you ever felt angry at God? What did you do with those feelings?

# 14
## The God to Whom We Pray

We have seen from the discussions and conversations at Trepolpen United Church that we can't go very far in thinking through questions about prayer until we face the much bigger problem of what we mean by 'God'. On this matter the house group produced a range of views. For Mary, God was 'Holy Mystery' or 'Spirit', active, alive and working in the world. For Geoff, God had to be 'in control.' For Clare, the minister, God was 'the one in whom we live and move and have our being'. Questions then arose about what, on each view, God can and cannot do, and these issues were also at the heart of the discussion at the Ministers' Fellowship. The time has come to explore them a bit further.

The Bible speaks of God as the Supreme Being, and the pictures it uses are overwhelmingly personal. Especially, but not exclusively, in the teaching of Jesus, God is described as 'Father'. Elsewhere he is addressed as 'King' and 'Lord', and also as 'Saviour', 'Redeemer', and 'Judge', which in the Bible's way of looking at things add up to the same thing. He is known, moreover, as 'Shepherd', 'Potter', our 'Maker' and the world's 'Creator'. But though these images clearly depict 'someone' rather than 'something', we are left in no doubt that, because God is 'spirit', his nature and being defy our imagination and our categories. We see this clearly in the opening phrase of the Lord's Prayer. Lest we forget that we are addressing one whose ways and thoughts are not ours, 'Our Father' is immediately qualified by 'who art in heaven'.

The two creeds reveal a similar approach. The Apostles Creed begins with, 'I believe in God, the Father almighty, creator of heaven and earth', and the Nicene Creed with, 'We believe in one God, the Father, the Almighty, maker of heaven and earth, of all that is, seen and unseen'. Both affirm that God is creator, one by speaking of 'creator of heaven and earth', the other by using the longer expression 'maker of heaven and earth, of all that is, seen and unseen'. Both also stress the unique power of God, calling him 'the Father almighty' and 'the Father, the Almighty'. In other words, the shorter creed uses 'almighty' as an adjective qualifying 'Father' in order to tell us what sort of a Father God is; the longer creed makes the same point by setting two descriptions, 'the Father' and 'the Almighty', alongside each other. In the Apostles Creed 'Almighty' translates the Latin term *omnipotentem* (as in 'omnipotent', all-powerful), and in the Nicene Creed it translates the equivalent Greek term *pantokratora*. As we have seen, the notion of 'omnipotence' – whether expressed in English, Latin or Greek – causes problems to which we must return later.

In a not very well-known hymn, Charles Wesley addresses God as 'Being of beings, God of love', phrases that remind us that, although personal images are the best we have with which to speak of God, they are not totally adequate. The value of 'Being of beings', for example, lies in the fact that it opens up the possibility of thinking of God as 'ultimate reality', and the whole hymn (*Hymns and Psalms* 690) is worth closer inspection. The opening phrase, 'Being of beings', points to the life behind all life and the reality behind all reality. It also provides a way of speaking about God in which Chrstians can join with people of other faiths and with believers who belong to no particular faith. For Christians, like many others, believe that the universe and all life within it is no accident, but that behind it, underneath it, in it, and through it there is an intelligence, a purpose, a reason and a personality which holds it all together. And the name they give to that ultimate reality is 'God'.

But in his hymn Charles Wesley goes on to say more, using the much warmer and user-friendly title, 'God of love', the core creed of the Old Testament which Jesus incarnates and the New Testament endorses. When we sing this hymn we are affirming that we believe the 'Being of beings', made known to us through the people of Israel and in Jesus Christ, to be a God of love. This is the God all Christians believe in and worship. If we ask what more we can say about him, the Bible offers us the key word, 'grace'. In the core creed of the Old Testament, for example, God is seen as a gracious God, one who is amazingly kind, generous and loving:

> a God merciful and gracious, slow to anger, and abounding in steadfast love and faithfulness, keeping steadfast love for the thousandth generation, forgiving iniquity and transgression and sin (Exodus 34.6–7).

The New Testament is convinced that Jesus expressed this grace of God in a unique way, that he actually embodied it:

> And the Word became flesh and lived among us, and we have seen his glory, the glory as of a father's only son, full of grace and truth... From his fullness we have all received, grace upon grace ... grace and truth came through Jesus Christ.' (John 1.14–17)

So, although the Bible insists that God cannot be named, defined or pictured, it speaks of him as the One who exists: the one 'in whom we live and move and have our being' (Acts 17.28), as Clare reminded Sue (chapter 10), and the 'Source, Guide and Goal of all that is', as the New English Bible translates Romans 11.36. This is the God about whom Jesus taught.

Subsequently Christianity went further, affirming that somehow this God was actually present in Jesus in a unique way and taking a first step towards the doctrine of 'The Trinity'. In the last verse of the hymn we have been exploring, Charles Wesley refers to the Father, the Son and the Holy Spirit, and the New Testament writers are happy to use those titles. But in neither case is any attempt made to weave them together into a theory. Rather, they are treated as handy ways of talking about how we experience God, the Being of beings and God of love. For we are, first and foremost, human beings, conscious of our lives as a gift and aware that the world to which we belong is no accident. We therefore speak of God as 'Father', or 'God the Father', or 'Creator', or even 'Mother', or the like. We are also Christians who have heard Jesus's message of love, felt something of his risen power and recognized in him the clue to the meaning of life. We therefore speak of him as the 'Son of God', or 'God the Son', or 'Lord', or 'Saviour', or the like. Moreover, we are believers and worshippers who know the presence of God as we pray and worship. We feel the touch of God as he comes to us through others or as he moves us and energizes us in the depths of our being. We are renewed as he gives us life and as we are caught up into God himself. We therefore speak of the 'Holy Spirit', or the 'Spirit of God', or the 'Spirit of Christ', or 'God the Holy Spirit', or the like.

In all these different ways we experience the presence of God with us, in us, and among us. But in every case it is the same God we experience, the one Being of beings, the one God of love. Wesley expresses the situation by speaking of Christians as 'made, and preserved, and saved' by this God. And in America there is a popular preference for talking of God as 'Creator, Redeemer and Sanctifier' rather than as 'Father, Son and Holy Spirit.' In both cases a range of experiences is related to the reality of the one God, and in the last verse of his hymn Charles Wesley adds a significant prayer:

> Come, Holy Ghost, the Saviour's love
> Shed in our hearts abroad;
> So shall we ever live, and move,
> And be with Christ in God'.

No doubt much more could, and some readers will say should, be made of the doctrine of the Trinity. But, at the very least, this picture or image of 'God in three persons, Blessed Trinity' suggests that the Ultimate Reality is not static but dynamic, that the Supreme Being is not to be likened to an isolated or solitary individual, and that the 'Godhead' is animated by the divine energy of love. We shall return to these ideas.

Before we leave this chapter, however, we must mention briefly the unnamed minister at the Ministers' Fellowship, who doesn't believe there is any thing or person – or even 'thing' or 'person' – 'out there', 'in there', 'behind there', or 'under there' to which we can apply the label 'God'. For him the word 'God' sums up the highest human values, and to 'believe in God' means to commit oneself to living by them and for them (chapter 11). This view is held, with integrity, by a number of today's Christians, though this is not the place to say more about it.

At the end of this chapter, it may be helpful, while bearing mind that when we talk about 'God' our language is strained to the utmost and that even the most fertile and agile imaginations can only glimpse the very outskirts of his ways, to attempt a definition of the God to whom we pray:

'God'
is
the Supreme Being or the Ultimate Reality;
best known as Father, Son and Spirit,
who is the Power behind the universe
and whose name and nature is love.

*Questions for discussion*

1. What would your thirty-word definition and description of God be? Or, if that question is too tough, how would you seek to define or describe God?

2. What do you think of the definition/description of God given above?

3. In what ways does Charles Wesley's hymn, 'Being of beings, God of love', describe the kind of God to whom we can pray?

# 15
## The God We Praise?

We have seen that thinking things through about prayer involves thinking things through about God, that there is more than one way in which Christians have understood God, and that all our words, phrases and ideas inevitably fall short because God is beyond description and beyond imagination. Moreover, bearing all this in mind, we came, at the end of the last chapter, to a tentative definition:

'God'
is
the Supreme Being or the Ultimate Reality;
best known as Father, Son and Spirit,
who is the Power behind the universe
and whose name and nature is love.

We also concluded, at the end of chapter 12, that prayer is:

the communication and communion, spoken and unspoken, that takes place between ourselves and God (in whatever terms we think of the Power behind the universe).

Again, it has been suggested that the basic dynamic of this communication and communion is the human need – individual and corporate – to give expression to our joy and our pain. And so, to close the circle, when we express these basic emotions we do not rejoice or cry into a void, but we direct our praise or our lament to or at God, the God who is there.

In the conversations at Trepolpen United Church it was the prayers of intercession which caused the most difficulty. What should Christians pray for? Does God respond to our requests and, if so, how does he do it? Does it make sense to speak of God 'acting', 'working', or 'doing things' at all? Geoff had no problems with the idea of God responding to requests,

Christine had many, and Mary and most of the others were somewhere in between. Although these questions came up most sharply when the group talked about prayers of intercession, they also arise in the case of prayers of adoration and thanksgiving.

*Adoration*

> Father, we adore you,
> Lay our lives before you;
> How we love you.

(In verses 2 and 3 'Jesus' and 'Spirit' are addressed.)

This simple, anonymous worship song from 1972 expresses the nature of adoration very well.

Some will criticize it for its very simplicity; but adoration is simple as love is simple. For God has made himself known to us in love, and adoration is our response to him in love. John Macquarrie, in the *Dictionary of Christian Spirituality,* says that the lines from Addison's hymn which we quoted in chapter 13 have got adoration about right, that it is being 'lost in wonder, love and praise' in the presence of absolute love.

It is usual for the first prayer in worship to be a prayer of adoration in which, as we gather in the presence of God and become conscious of his glory, goodness and love, we focus on God, sometimes by saying the sort of thing that this worship song expresses, sometimes by saying nothing at all. To adore God may be to say, 'We are here because we love you. We love you because you are the kind of God you are' (Susan White). Or it may be to obey the injunction, 'Be still and know that I am God'. Or it may be to repeat the opening part of the Lord's Prayer, 'Our Father who art in heaven, hallowed be thy name'. To adore is to focus our complete attention on God in gratitude and in openness to his presence, to be with him as he is with us.

Sometimes writers who talk about adoration use the analogy of human love. They point out that lovers adore each other, that they are more than happy simply to be in each other's company and that they may or may not need to talk. This analogy has one obvious weakness when applied to our relationship to God – whereas lovers adore each other, God loves us but does not adore us – but if we allow for this, it does have something to say.

Adoration arises out of the dynamic of praise. It is one way of expressing a 'Yes' to our experience of the love of God. We are not thanking him in any way in adoration, either for what he is or for what he has done. That will come later in the prayers of thanksgiving. In adoration we respond to the hymnwriter's exhortation, 'O worship the Lord in the beauty of holiness . . . Kneel and adore him: the Lord is his name.' Why? Because to focus upon God as he is is uniquely satisfying.

But at this point someone observing our worship with a cynical eye, or overhearing our prayers of adoration with a suspicious ear may ask: 'What does this do to God or for God?' 'What sort of a god is this', they may say, 'who seems to want to be flattered every time his people meet in worship? Or who needs to be adored, to be constantly told how much he is loved and how great he is?' 'Isn't this', they may suggest, 'the sort of homage which a despot with an insecurity complex needs to receive from fawning subjects?' At the very least this kind of question sounds a warning that here is one more place where our language falls short. If God is somehow 'personal', a 'Supreme Being' in our definition of God, then our ways of speaking to him in adoration are open to misrepresentation.

The Christian reply, of course, is that God does not ask for flattery, and that in adoration no flattery is offered. We have already referred to the analogy between our relationship with God and the relationship of two lovers. Where the lovers are concerned, neither party demands adoration from the other, and if one or other did, we would judge that there was something seriously wrong with the relationship. And where God is concerned, to suggest that he demands adoration is to reveal that, in his case, some analogies are better than others! I suspect, in fact, that few people do think that prayers of adoration are about telling God how good he is because that's what he wants to hear. But the very fact that the suggestion can be made shows that some ways of speaking about God can create more problems than they solve.

Adoration, especially when no words are used but candles are lit or icons contemplated, is a form of spirituality which seems to be increasingly popular outside the churches. It is part of an explosion of interest in religion in the western world at a time when traditional forms of church life appear to be connecting with fewer and fewer people. It is a response to the mystery and glory which gleam and resound through all creation, and many find it a helpful way of praying, in terms of what it does to them and for them. It provides a way of centring down, of receiving energy, of focusing, of communing with God or with one's inner self or, as some people put it, of simply chilling out, and the personal benefits of this type of prayer are clear. It also fits well with that part of our definition of prayer which speaks of prayer as communion between ourselves and God – in whatever terms we may think of the power behind the universe.

*Thanks*

> For life and love, for rest and food,
>   For daily help and nightly care,
> Sing to the Lord, for he is good,
>   And praise his name, for it is fair.

(J. S. B. Monsell (1811–1875), 'Sing to the Lord a joyful song', verse 2 (*Hymns and Psalms* 17))

Thanksgiving also arises out of the dynamic of praise. Prayers of thanks affirm the giftedness of life and respond to it with a grateful 'Yes!' If you wake on a bright spring morning, glimpse a glorious Cornish country scene through the bedroom window, and look forward to a good breakfast and a fulfilling day's work ahead, what else can you say except 'Praise the Lord!' But what if you wake somewhere else? In less comfortable circumstances? With no prospect of a meal at all? Without home, health, or security? Shall we then sing hymns like this quite so readily? I suspect, from observation and experience, that if British Christians might not, African Christians would! So there is a warning here to begin with, that too many of our prayers of thanksgiving tend to be twee, romantic and self-focused.

> We bless thee for our creation, preservation and all the blessings of this life; but above all for thine inestimable love in the redemption of the world by our Lord Jesus Christ; for the means of grace, and for the hope of glory.
> (The General Thanksgiving in *The Book of Common Prayer*.)

Note the extra dimension added here, that of God's redeeming work and of our future hope. This is an important feature of many prayers of thanksgiving, not least the Thanksgiving in the service of Holy Communion in which we thank God 'for all he has given us, especially for our salvation in Christ'.

'Praise and thanksgiving', gratitude and appreciation, are clearly good things: but behind this seemingly innocent type of prayer lies a much more serious problem than the rose-coloured words we sometimes use in saying them. It might be too simple to say that Adoration focuses on who God is and Thanksgiving on what he has done, but that distinction is often made and it is a helpful one. This means that the huge question of 'providence' – of what God does or doesn't do, what he can or can't do, and how he actually does it, if he does anything at all – is raised, not quite so starkly as in prayers of intercession but raised none the less, by prayers of thanksgiving.

73

Previous generations of Christians had little problem with the idea of providence. They happily sang hymns which said, 'His providence has brought us through another various year' (Charles Wesley), and, 'Thy providence is kind and large, Both man and beast thy bounty share' (Isaac Watts) from a Methodist Hymn Book which had a section headed 'God: In Creation and Providence'. Donald Hughes, a twentieth-century hymn-writer, has given us an update of this in:

> O Father, whose creating hand
> Brings harvest from the fruitful land,
> Your providence we gladly own.

God was, our forebears believed, the Creator of the world who continued to sustain it, and for this they used the term 'general providence'. God had, they believed, created everything in such a way that it all worked for the best, with humanity at the centre of things benefiting from God's generous provision.

They recognized, of course, that sin had entered in and fouled things up considerably, with the result that humanity did not always enjoy the fullness of life which God had intended and for which he had provided. He had provided enough food for all, for example, but greed or sloth had resulted in disparities between rich and poor. They also believed, however, in the 'special providence' of God, who could and did intervene to right wrongs, answer prayer, and help people or communities in special need. They saw that the Bible was full of examples of God's special providence: in blessing his ancient people of Israel, in sending his Son to redeem the world, in enabling Christ and the apostles to perform miracles, and in wonderfully meeting the needs of the early Christians. They believed in a God who acted, not just once in the creation of the world, nor just generally in keeping the world in being, but in particular times, places and ways as he saw fit. Prayers of intercession fitted easily and naturally into this way of believing. They were ways of asking God to do something for you or for the person for whom you prayed. Prayers of thanksgiving were the way you said 'Thank you' after he had done it. For many Christians today, like Geoff, this way of looking at God poses few problems.

Perhaps this is the point to come back to our analogies, our images and pictures of God. Speaking of God as 'Creator' obviously links in to our definition of him as the 'Supreme Being'. It also suggests, however, that he stands outside of and distinct from his creation, just as a maker is distinct from what he has made, no matter how much of himself he has put into the making of it. Such a Maker can, Geoff would argue, tweak what he has made to make it work better, or fix bits here and there as needed. In this way of looking at things, science can help us to see how the product usually works and how things normally operate, but science itself is not an 'exact science' and hasn't yet been able to understand everything. And we know, from the Bible and our own experiences, that amazing things do happen in this world which God has made. So one day, when we know more, we shall be able to understand the mechanisms by which God, the Maker, continues to tweak what he has made. This is the way the argument can unfold if you begin from the 'Supreme Being equals Maker' analogy.

For people like Christine, however, this way of thinking poses huge problems, especially the idea of God's 'special providence'. We heard the house group debating the issues. If God can intervene, then why doesn't he in this or that case? Why does he choose to do so in some cases but not in others? Can he intervene at all? How can God, who is 'spirit', affect material things? How does talk of God intervening relate to what we know about the realities of life through science? How can God affect the weather, heal the sick, or provide a car-parking space when all of these areas of life seem to work according to principles we can map out and explain?

For many Christians today these are serious issues about the world as it is and about the nature of God, which call in question traditional belief in 'Providence'. For them, the 'Ultimate Reality' or 'Power behind the universe' analogy, offers better possibilities of making sense of these things. In this way of thinking – Christine and the minister's way – God is not separate from the universe in the way that a maker is separate from what is made. Instead, God is the power and energy within everything, intimately and indivisibly involved in creation, sustaining it, energizing it and moving it on, just as the idea of 'general providence' has traditionally said. Gratitude and thanksgiving are appropriate emotions, therefore, because there is much worth appreciating and thanking God for in this evolving universe of which he is 'source, guide and goal'. There is little place, however, for 'miracles' and 'special providence' in this way of looking at things.

*Questions for discussion*

1. How can we avoid our prayers of thanksgiving being 'twee, romantic, and self-focused?

2. What place is left for adoration and thanksgiving in a world in which there is so much pain and nature can be described as 'red in tooth and claw'?

3. 'God our maker doth provide, For our wants to be supplied' seems to be the logic behind prayers of thanksgiving. If God 'provides', how do you think that he does so?

# 16
## The God Who Forgives?

This chapter can be brief, for while all kinds of questions can be asked about forgiveness itself, prayers of confession and declarations of forgiveness present few problems.

Let us confess our sins in penitence and faith, firmly resolved to keep God's commandments and to live in love and peace with all.

Most merciful God,
Father of our Lord Jesus Christ,
we confess that we have sinned
in thought, word and deed.
We have not loved you with our whole heart.
We have not loved our neighbours as ourselves.
In your mercy,
forgive what we have been,
help us to amend what we are,
and direct what we shall be;
that we may do justly,
love mercy,
and walk humbly with you, our God.
Amen.

So reads the confession from the first service of Holy Communion in *Common Worship – Services and Prayers for the Church of England,* and the worship books of other mainline churches have something similar.

*The Methodist Worship Book* follows its prayer of confession with this declaration of forgiveness,

If we confess our sins,
God is faithful and just

and will forgive our sins,
and cleanse us from all unrighteousness.
Amen. Thanks be to God.


Confession arises out of the dynamic of lament, from a sense of our own failure and of the shortcomings of our world. It is rooted in our acknowledgement of things wrongly done or left undone, of the distance between the world as it is and the world as it should be, and of the gap between who we are and who we could be. And it expresses our awareness of distance from God, our conviction that we are 'sinners'. Almost inevitably, the textbooks tell us, confession follows adoration. For when, after contemplating the grandeur of God, the beauty of his holiness, the purity of his love, and the generosity of his kindness, we look at ourselves and our fellows, we cannot be happy with what we see. So we turn to God in penitence, admitting what we are and seeking his forgiveness,

This is not the place to discuss sin, but its nature can be indicated by a simple catechism:

Q. What is sin?
A. Sin is the condition of estrangement from God which affects the whole human race. Sins are specific actions, words or thoughts which arise from our sinful condition and deny the presence, power and purpose of God.
Q. What are the effects of sin?
A. Sin hinders the effects of God's grace. It corrupts our relationship with him and with one another, with the world we live in and with ourselves. The effect of sin is discord, where God intended harmony.


We can be content with that. There is no doubt that the effects of 'sin' are obvious enough and that they can be terrible. At the same time, however, I rather share the view, which used to be more popular than it seems to be now, that Christianity overdoes its preoccupation with sin. And I certainly think that the inclusion of confession in every service and in every prayer can be counter-productive and lead to a trivialization of sin.

The bottom line, however, is that sin needs to be dealt with, and prayers of confession are a key factor. For, if you accept the basic Christian conviction that God forgives all those who repent, then confession is the way of voicing that repentance, and the assurance of forgiveness which follows is the way of hearing that our sins are forgiven. And we certainly know how confession 'works' from the human end. Giving voice to those things which are causing pain inside, the psychologists tell us, is a good way of dealing with them. Speaking-it-out, therefore, is a very common form of therapy which releases the pain and makes new self-understanding possible, and much of the counselling industry is built on this simple truth. In short, prayers of confession are theologically unproblematic and therapeutically effective, even if they may need a health warning against over-prescription.

## *Questions for discussion*

1. What do you think is the effect of being called to confess our sin in every service of worship?

2. Some Christian traditions encourage private confession to a priest. Others view the practice with suspicion. What do you think?

3. This chapter argues that there are no theological problems with prayers of confession and that they are helpful and effective. What do you think?

# 17
## The God Who Acts?

This is the crunch issue, about which opinions at Trepolpen United Church were most divided, and it comes out most clearly in their discussions of prayers of intercession. In intercession we express to God both our concern for others and our own needs. This type of prayer arises from the dynamic of lament, from those situations in which, because things are not as they ought to be, a 'No' is wrung from us and we seek relief, for ourselves and others.

Intercession is, for many, the most difficult kind of prayer to think through. Paradoxically, however, it is probably the kind of prayer most frequently offered. Think of all those people who light candles in Cathedrals, write names on Prayer Boards or in Intercession Books, and mention individuals in times of open prayer. Even those at Trepolpen United Church who can't believe in a 'God who acts' or 'intervenes' still consider it important to 'hold people before God' and say to friends in need that they will 'think of them in their prayers'.

This is where the crucial questions – whether or not God can act and why, if he can, he does or doesn't – come into sharpest focus. Here is where the 'problem of unanswered prayer' rears its head, though the 'problem of answered prayer' is really just as acute. Why did God do something here but not there?

The way through this maze is by going back to our analogies or pictures of God.

There is, on the face of it, much to be said for thinking of God as the 'Supreme Being'. The Bible pictures him in this way, and, by describing him especially as 'Our Father who art in Heaven', makes it easier to relate to him personally, as a child would to a parent. It also makes it possible to speak to him as to a friend, and there are many hymns and prayers which do just that. According to this way of thinking, intercession is to be understood as asking this Friend for something which he is able to give but also has the right to withhold. For if he is Sovereign, he has 'sovereign freedom' to do as he wills. His answers to prayer, therefore, may be 'Yes', 'No', 'Wait' or 'Not in the Way you Expect'. Question 39 in the *Methodist Catechism* asks, 'Does God always hear our prayers?' and answers,

God always hears our prayers, but does not always answer immediately or in the way we expect. Or he may answer, and we fail to realize he has done so. Or we may be the means by which God answers our own prayers or those of others.

Needless to say, there are practices which, for many people, undermine the credibility of this way of understanding intercession – for example, the long prayer meeting in which the same requests are repeated again and again, as though God's reluctance to oblige has to be worn down. But if we picture God in personal terms and think of a person, as the Catechism tends to do, as someone who can do things, there is here a possible way of understanding intercession, based on the twin beliefs that 'God is in control' and that 'God knows best'. Many Christians have no difficulty with this rationale.

For others, however, it is problematic. They find themselves asking two questions about Geoff's fundamental belief that 'God is in control': Is he really? and How does he exercise such control? They cannot sing the chorus which says, 'There is nothing my God cannot do'. In short, they have difficulty with the doctrine of the omnipotence of God. Like me, they may be uncomfortable when God is addressed, as he so often is in worship, as 'Almighty God'.

For them, all the facts of life tell against such an idea. Or, if it is true that God is almighty, he cannot be said to be loving or caring. In other words, they feel the full force of the age-old challenge – that the character of the world appears incompatible with the claim that God is both all-powerful and all-good. It seems, therefore, that if they are to hold to their fundamental belief that God is good, they have at least to modify the idea that God is in control.

Such modification is not new. Christians of previous generations have used several analogies to express the view that God is not in total control. They have suggested, for example, that God may be more like a creative artistic director, who is able to bring different actors, music and plot into focus as a production develops and unfolds. Or he may resemble a painter who is able to make something of those colours and brush-strokes that didn't quite work first time by working them into a new picture. At the very least, traditional theology has recognized that God gives space to his creation and freewill to human beings. This may result in men and women acting as he would not wish and, in the process, creating mayhem for themselves, for others and for the environment. But that is the price of freedom. And, some have argued, if he gives that kind of freedom to one set of his 'creatures', he presumably does the same to others – like the angels and archangels or the 'principalities and powers', whose misuse of the gift may have even more catastrophic effects on life than ours. Either way, God is not in 'total control' of the present, even if the final outcome may not be in doubt. Others, moreover, may want to go further. They may prefer to say that, since the universe is evolving, the future is genuinely open, and, though God is involved in the process, the whole idea of 'control' or the lack of it is not the most helpful way of thinking about this issue.

That God is not in control may be, for some, a frightening suggestion. For in a world as dangerous as ours the idea that God is in control and that one day he will finally work out his purposes and make everything come right is a last defence against despair and hopelessness. The alternative, a world spinning out of control or just going on aimlessly with no direction and purpose, may be just too frightening to contemplate. The view that Good and Evil are battling for control may be equally unacceptable, either because it looks too much like the theme of a computer game or because it expresses the old heresy of 'dualism' in a new form. To some, however, it may seem to offer, on the basis of a realistic assessment, an invitation to a more courageous faith. For, in the context of a cosmic struggle of good against evil, our actions, our lifestyles, our decisions, and our prayers of intercession have a clear meaning and purpose.

If, then, you find belief that 'God is in control' untenable or are unable to believe that God can manage the weather, arrange car-parking spaces, and heal June's daughter of an inoperable cancer, perhaps the other analogy offers a better way forward.

It begins from the assumption that God, as Ultimate Reality and Power behind the Universe, is always and everywhere at work and that his ongoing task is to make all things new, redeeming and restoring in love what forces of evil and sin are continually spoiling. This divine energy is always 'for' us, and so there is never any sense of God having to be persuaded to 'hear our prayer'.

Intercession, on this understanding, is adding our concern, our compassion and the energy of our love to what God is already doing. It is focused on giving, the giving of ourselves in this loving work, rather than on receiving, the receiving of a benefit or a result. And the effect of this giving cannot be measured. Who knows what 'miracles' and 'marvels' are achieved in against-the-odds situations by such outpoured and committed compassion? But we cannot collate or assess results. There is no formula allowing us to calculate that so much intercessory energy will result in such and such a change of circumstances. And in that sense the question of 'answered' or 'unanswered' prayer becomes irrelevant, just as 'asking' for something specific for oneself or for someone else begins to look inappropriate.

This approach is very close to that offered by Neville Ward in his classic *The Use of Praying*, where he speaks of intercession as God's invitation, indeed his 'summons', to us to join in his ongoing work. This way of understanding intercession, like that based on requests to a Friend, is vulnerable to unfortunate practices – for example, long lists of people or places through which the preacher seems to be informing God, demonstrating his or her own breadth of 'compassion', and manipulating the congregation. But it illustrates the fact that, if you change the metaphor about God, other things will also change, some of them, as in this case, for the better.

Like private intercession, especially when enriched by suitable aids, corporate intercessory prayer, whichever way we understand it, has quite practical spin-offs. It raises consciousness, widens horizons, stimulates action and creates community as it enables individuals to grow in grace, knowledge and love. And such effects are far from being mere fringe-benefits. Archbishop William Temple put it like this: 'We do not pray in order to change God's will, but to bring our wills into harmony with his'.

Another way of putting it is the affirmation – not a biblical text! – which you can see on some posters: 'Prayer changes people, and people change things'. For some Christians, like Geoff, this will be inadequate and they will want to say a lot more about intercession and probably about all prayer. For others this aphorism will express most of what they are able to say with integrity. For them it is not a trite little slogan on a poster, but a profoundly true statement of how prayer 'works'.

*Questions for discussion*

1. How do you understand the two descriptions of God as 'Ultimate Reality' and 'Supreme Being'? In what ways does each of them affect our view of prayer?

2. What do you think about the suggestions that God might not be 'in control'?

3. Can you improve on 'releasing energy and compassion' as a way of thinking about intercessory prayer?

4. How would you describe the way prayer works?

5. What issues about prayer has this book helped you to think through?

# Further Reading

*A Catechism for the use of the people called Methodists* (Methodist Publishing House, 1986, updated in 2000).

Seventy questions asked and answered.

R. E. Clements, *The Prayers of the Bible* (SCM Press, 1985).

After an introductory chapter on 'Prayer in the Bible', this older book looks at twenty-five prayers in the Bible, excluding the Psalter and Lamentations, and comments on each one.

Robert Davidson, *The Courage to Doubt* (SCM Press, 1983).

A classic book which explores those Old Testament passages which question God, doubt his lovingkindness, and demand a faith big enough to look at life as it is.

C. S. Rodd, *Thinking Things Through 4: Why Evil and Suffering?* (Epworth Press, 2000).

Using the format of this series, this book engages with the most pressing of all pastoral questions.

C. S. Rodd, *Thinking Things Through 9: Is There a God?* (Epworth Press, 2002).

Using the format of this series, this book raises the crucial questions and discusses the various responses to them traditionally and currently made.

Marjorie J. Thompson, *Soul Feast* (Westminster John Knox Press, 1995).

This book is 'an invitation to the Christian spiritual life', which introduces the reader to spiritual reading, prayer, fasting, self-examination, spiritual direction, and, unusually, hospitality. It is a 'how to' book which does not neglect the 'why?' questions.

Michael E. W. Thompson, *The Old Testament and Prayer* (Epworth Press, 1996).

This book ends with a chapter on 'Old Testament Prayer', after looking at all the ways in which prayer is offered in the Old Testament, including, crucially, careful consideration of prayer in the Book of Psalms.

Gordon S. Wakefield, editor, *A Dictionary of Christian Spirituality* (SCM Press, 1983).

SCM Press did us all a great service by producing its 'Dictionaries' in the 1980s and 1990s. This one still remains an important resource.

J. Neville Ward, *The Use of Praying* (Epworth Press, 1967).

This is a classic on prayer. Written by a Methodist minister, now dead, this book gives guidance to those who would grow in the life of prayer as well as offering a searching critique of the whole enterprise.

Fraser Watts, editor, *Perspectives on Prayer* (SPCK, 2001).

This book comprises a series of lectures by various distinguished Cambridge Christians on 'Prayer and ... ', and contains fascinating perspectives on Prayer and the Bible, Society, Science, Psychology, Poetry, Music, Sexuality, and the Body.

Maurice Wiles, *God's Action in the World* (SCM Press, 1986).

These are the Bampton Lectures for 1986 dealing with the huge question at the heart of any discussion about prayer, especially prayers of intercession. Professor Wiles asks: Does God act in the world? Does he affect what happens to us in the varied experiences of daily life? If so, in what ways and by what means?